Here is an arm-chair expedition into various world cultures, an imaginary field-trip that reveals different views of autonomy, concepts of the individual in his society, interpretations of personal freedom.

Dorothy Lee brings Wintu, Hopi, Tikopia, Trobriand, and many other cultures into focus, often contrasting them with our social structure, delineating the differences in language patterns, responsibilities as citizens of a community, the appreciation of individual expression.

The point of view of this work, a unique perspective on these contemporary materials, is achieved through Dorothy Lee's ability to fuse the anthropologist's contact with many cultures and a personal concern with the immediate responsibilities of citizenship, homelife, and motherhood. The result is a blending of science and the humanities—a readable, warm, and concrete account of freedom, being, and existence. The way this material is related to immediate situations—such as the education of children and the meaning and use of "free time"—will provide a lift to the creative imagination of readers concerned with these matters.

Dorothy Lee is Greek by birth. She was educated, married, and is raising her children, in America. She has lectured throughout the country, held positions at Vassar College and the Merrill-Palmer School. She is currently Lecturer in Anthropology and Research Anthropologist at Harvard University.

Freedom and Culture

DOROTHY LEE
Harvard University

A SPECTRUM  BOOK
PRENTICE-HALL, INC.

L. C. Cat. Card No.: 59-15584

Printed in the United States of America
3 3 0 4 9 — C

Current printing (last digit):
25 24 23 22 21 20 19 18

Preface

THE PAPERS IN THIS VOLUME WERE selected, arranged, and edited by my friends Clark Moustakas and David Smillie. It was they who saw unity in my scattered publications of the last fifteen years, they who undertook the painstaking work of preparing the manuscript and of attending to the many details involved. By their decision, their names do not appear on the title page; yet they are largely responsible for this book, since without their encouragement and appreciation and hard work the volume would not have appeared.

The individual papers themselves owe much to my hundreds of students at Vassar College and The Merrill-Palmer School; to my students whose fresh vision, whose goading questions, whose uncluttered insights, whose refusal to accept what I took for granted, helped me to break through the wall of my presuppositions, and to pursue a new idea along its tortuous way.

The original impetus to inquire into the philosophical dimension of culture came from my husband, Otis Lee, for whom all experience and behavior had its philosophical content, and all reality held value. My search into the cultural codification of experienced reality, and into the conceptual and value implications of language and other aspects of culture, came through an attempt to find answers for his disturbing questions.

In recent years, I have been concerned with questions revolving around freedom, individual autonomy, responsibility, creativity, the self. My many friends have helped me in this inquiry; in particular I am indebted to Clark Moustakas, David Smillie, Abraham Maslow, Frances Wilson Schwarz, Nancy Morse Samelson, and David Riesman.

To Anna, Mary, Ronald, and Sabra

who walk through these pages

Contents

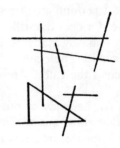

Introduction

THE COMMON THEME OF THE ESSAYS in this volume is that culture is a symbolic system which transforms the physical reality, what is *there*, into experienced reality. It follows from this assumption that the universe as I know it or imagine it in the Western world is different from the universe of the Tikopia, in Polynesia. It follows, also, that I feel differently about what I see. As I look out of my window now, I see trees, some of which I like to be there, and some of which I intend to cut down to keep them from encroaching further upon the small clearing I made for my house. The Dakota Black Elk Indian, however, saw trees as having rights to the land, equal to his own. He saw them as the "standing peoples, in whom the winged ones built their lodges and reared their families."

In cultural behavior, I see a system whereby the self is related to the universe—the relevant universe in each case, whether society, nature, the known universe, or ultimate reality. The individual acts within each culturally structured situation would then be expressions of this relatedness. The breaking of the soil in the agricultural process may be an act of vio-

1

lence, of personal aggression, of mastery, of exploitation, of self-fulfilment; or it may be an act of tender fostering, of involvement in the processes of the earth, of helping the land to bring forth in its due time; it may be an act of worship, and the field an altar.

According to the conceptual framework of my culture, I perceive my own behavior differently from the way in which people of another cultural framework view theirs. And which of these is the true way? When I throw a ball, do I perform an aggressive causal act, as my culture predisposes me to believe? Or does the ball leave my hand, as the Greenland Eskimo puts it, or do I merely actualize the ball's potential to move, as the Navaho would have it? These are different ways of perceiving the same situation, but which is the truth? Are they all true, all different facets of the same truth?

I turn to the study of other cultures largely to answer this question. I believe that these are all different codifications of the same reality, and different responses in terms of these codifications. My own culture, with its laws of logic, its principles of cognition, its rigidly defined limits of validation, offers me a strongly bounded and precategorized view of reality. This is one way of perceiving; it is a finite way—yet reality, itself, I believe to be infinite.

When I study other cultures, I find a different codification, I get a different glimpse of reality, from a different starting point. I find other, equally self-consistent systems of symbolization, with diametrically opposed principles of validation of experience. Thus I am enabled to some extent to go beyond my own finite view; I am enabled to see my culture as one of many possible systems of relating the self to the universe, and to question tenets and axioms of which I had never been aware.

I do not mean in any sense that I consider myself to be a captive within my culture, or that I am an automaton whose experience and behavior were determined for me. Neither do I agree with those social scientists who hold that culture is inhibiting and frustrating in nature. Cultures may inhibit to a greater or lesser degree; but I believe that generally speaking, culture offers a guide to the individual, and possibly provides limits within which the individual can function in his own way.

To make clear what I mean, I shall speak of one aspect of culture to which we have all been formally exposed—language. A language is full of regulations and interdictions; yet it is freeing. Through learning the rules, I am enabled to communicate with others, I am free to express myself and often to achieve ends which I could not otherwise reach. I am not hampered by the rigid taboo against using a singular verb for a plural subject; I am not outraged when I am commanded to add *ed* to *wash* when I refer to yesterday. And I do not feel that all my originality is submerged through the need to conform to regulations.

Certainly our great writers are those who are intimately acquainted with all the rules of the language, and who have internalized these and all the innumerable taboos pertaining to the use of our large vocabulary. Within this highly structured system, Shakespeare and T. S. Eliot have achieved their own peculiar styles, and the expression of one could never be confused with that of the other.

Perhaps the most difficult work the anthropologist has to do is to make his way into another codification of reality. It is difficult to realize that what we know about human nature, about motivation, about emotions, about satisfactions is not necessarily true of all human beings, but may be true only of the human beings who have been brought up within our own cultural framework. When we see the behavior of people of a different culture, it is difficult to refrain from making automatically our usual assumptions as to their motives. When we read about another culture, we have to remember to read every word; we have to forget our habits of fast reading, because, when we begin a sentence, we can never predict what its end will be.

Every one of the brief cultural descriptions I have given in this volume represents the work of years. In reading accounts of a culture, I examine each described act carefully and repeatedly, trying to eliminate the bias and categories of the reporting ethnographer until I can uncover each situation as it occurred. Only then can I begin to search for the meaning of the act to the actor; and only then can I try to discover how the situation is culturally shaped and presented to the experiencing individual.

To make this inquiry, I have worked minutely with each culture, over a period of years. I have paid attention even to apparently irrelevant detail, until some item struck a resonant note. I have then gone back and forth in my reading, seeing new relevance, noticing the obscure or seemingly trite or obvious. I have done this until nothing remained queer any more, and little seemed inexplicable. At this point I made tentative predictions as to what I should find in the linguistic structure, and in the mythology. If these predictions were confirmed, I went back to the descriptive account, strengthened in my conclusions and with my vision sharpened, and then I went to the language with the search for further confirmation. This process occupied much time; but even apart from the time-consuming work, I found that the process of understanding a radically different codification of reality was one of long duration, one of waiting until the acquaintance ripened and the bewildering and contradictory became clear and simple.

Eventually, I plunged into the experience of another culture, until I found myself liking what the members of the other society liked, frightened by what gave them fear, grieved by their sorrows, delighted in the situations which filled them with satisfaction and joy; and until their categories seemed natural and right, and my own rigid and misleading. In fact, I sometimes lost myself in the way of life of the society I was studying until my children complained that, after all, they were not Trobrianders or Tikopia! What I had to say seemed so obvious to me that, at this point, I could bring myself to write at all only by reminding myself that I was writing for people who were ignorant of this particular culture.

This approach is the common basis of whatever unity there is in this volume.

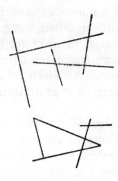

Individual Autonomy
and Social Structure

RESPECT FOR INDIVIDUAL INTEGRITY, for what we have called human dignity, has long been a tenet in American culture, and it is certainly no novel principle to anyone working in the area of interpersonal relations. However, in a heterogeneous society such as ours, and in an era of induced change and speeded tempo of living, it has been difficult to implement this tenet in the everyday details of living. We have to reconcile principles of conformity and individual initiative, group living and private freedom of choice, social regulation and personal autonomy. I believe that a study of other societies dealing with such issues in different circumstances can furnish us with insights which we can use in understanding our own situation. So I present here scattered material from a number of societies, ending with a brief sketch of the culture of the Navaho Indians, to show how the principle of personal autonomy is supported by the cultural framework.

In every society we find some organized social unit; but not everywhere does the social unit provide freedom to the individual or the opportunity for spontaneous functioning; nor do we find everywhere the value for sheer personal being of which I shall speak below. We often find a hier-

From *Personnel and Guidance Journal*, 1956.

archy where women or children or the uninitiated or the commoners are accorded a minority status. In some societies we find what amounts to a dictatorship; in others, the group may demand such sacrifice of individual uniqueness as to make for totalitarianism. On the other hand, in some societies we encounter a conception of individual autonomy and democratic procedures which far outstrip anything we have practiced or even have conceived of as democracy. It is only the latter kind which concerns me here.

It is often difficult for us to decide exactly how much our principle of personal autonomy involves. We find ourselves asking questions such as: to what extent can we allow a child to make his own decisions, to speak and act for himself? And: at what point do we begin to allow him to do so? For example, obviously when the mother first takes her infant to the pediatrician, she has to speak for him. Exactly when does she begin to remain silent, waiting for him to understand and answer the doctor's questions and to express his own likes and opinions and conclusions? And to what extent can she do this, using up the time of her appointment, taking up the valuable time of a busy physician?

Many of us feel that to allow a child to decide for himself and to act according to his own wish, that is, to be permissive, is to show respect for the unique being of the child. Yet for many of the societies we know, it would be presumption for any person to "allow" another to take what is essentially his prerogative—the right to decide for himself. These people do not "permit" others. When their children, as for example the children of the Wintu Indians, ask "Can I?" they are asking for information on the rules of the structure; for instance, they may be seeking clarification about a religious taboo or a social custom. They are saying in effect, "Is it permissible for me to . . . ?" and not, "Do you allow me to . . . ?" These people do not "give" freedom to their children, because it is not theirs to give. If they do not impose an external time schedule on their infants, but feed them when they are hungry, and put them to bed when they are sleepy, they are not being "permissive"; they are showing their deep-seated respect for individual worth, and their awareness of the unique tempo of the individual.

Ethnographers have presented us with many incidents, apparently commonplace and trivial, which point out for us an amazingly thoroughgoing implementation of respect for personal quality. For instance, Marian Smith tells how, when she was visiting a Sikh household in British Columbia, she noticed that a small child, asked to entertain his baby brother, merely went up to the playpen and put in a toy truck. He did not show the baby how the truck worked, how he could make the wheels go round; he gave the truck silently. This amazed the visitor, since she knew that the Sikhs were people of great empathy and warmth, and with a great love for babies. She knew, also, that the child in question had approached the baby with friendliness and affection. Yet, under similar circumstances an American child would probably have told the baby what to look for. Then she remembered the personal autonomy of the Sikh, and realized that the boy was acting consistently with the cultural values; he was furnishing the baby with the raw material for experience, and leaving him to explore and discover for himself, without any attempt to influence him. He was expressing respect, not non-involvement.

Such respect for autonomy may appear extreme to us, yet it would be taken for granted in a number of the Indian tribes in this continent. For example, an anthropology student who was observing relations between parents and children was puzzled to see a baby with hair so long that it got in his eyes and seemed to cause him discomfort, though otherwise his mother treated him with care and affection. When she finally asked why the baby's hair had been left so long, the mother answered, "He has not asked to have it cut." The baby was about eighteen months old, and could barely talk; yet the mother would not take it upon herself to act for him without his request or consent.

These instances exemplify a belief so deep that it apparently permeates behavior and decisions, and operates without question or reflection or conscious plan. It is a belief so internalized as to be regarded as almost an organic ingredient of the personality. The individual, shown absolute respect from birth and valued as sheer being for his own uniqueness, apparently learns with every experience to have this same respect and value for others; he is "trained" to be constantly sensitive to the beginnings of others.

An instance of this "training" in sensitivity comes from the culture of the Chinese. American observers had noticed that Chinese babies had learned, by the time they were about six months old, to indicate that they wanted to micturate; yet they seemed to be treated very permissively, with no attempt at toilet training. A Chinese mother explained that there actually is such "training"; only it is the mother who "trains" herself. When the baby wants to urinate, his whole body participates in the preliminary process. The Chinese mother, holding the baby in her arms, learns to be sensitive to the minute details of this process, and to hold her baby away from herself at exactly the critical moment. Eventually, the infant learns to ask to be held out. The mother neither tries to control the baby, nor does she train the infant to control himself according to imposed standards. Instead, she sensitizes herself to his rhythm, and helps him to adopt social discipline with spontaneity, starting from his unique pattern. What is interesting here is that as an end result of this, the baby is "toilet-trained" at a very early age; but it has been an experience of spontaneity for him and his autonomy has remained inviolate, because his mother has had the sensitivity and the patience to "listen" to him.

Among the Wintu Indians of California, the principle of the inviolate integrity of the individual is basic to the very morphology of the language. Many of the verbs which express coercion in our language—such as to take a baby to (the shade), or to change the baby—are formed in such a way that they express a cooperative effort instead. For example, the Wintu would say, "I *went with* the baby," instead of, "*I took* the baby." And they say, "The chief *stood with* the people," which they have to translate into English as, "The chief ruled the people." They never say, and in fact they cannot say, as we do, "I have a sister," or a "son," or "husband." Instead, they say, "I am sistered," or "I live with my sister." *To live with* is the usual way in which they express what we call possession, and they use this term for everything that they respect, so that a man will be said to live with his bow and arrows. In our society, when we try to express respect for individual uniqueness, we have to do it in so many words, and even then we have to grapple with an uncooperative language. This is why we have to resort to terms which actually defeat our ends; terms such as *permissiveness*, or phrases such as *to give freedom to the child*. In Wintu, every interpersonal reference is couched in grammar which rests on the principle of individual integrity. Yet, for this people, the emphasis on personal inviolability did not mean that the individual was an isolate. There was such pervasive empathy among them that this, too, was expressed in the grammatical forms; if a boy was sick, the father used a special form of the verb phrase *to be sick*, and thus said, "I-am-sick-in-respect-of-my-son."

A corollary of the principle of individual integrity is that no personal orders can be given or taken without a violation of personal autonomy; we have been familiar with this corollary, particularly in rural areas where the farmer and his wife had "help" but not "servants." In a society such as that of Upper Burma before it was much affected by Western administration, there were no agricultural laborers nor household help at all. In the monasteries, where novices performed menial tasks, the monks did not give orders. Instead, the work was structured throughout the day; and all that the monk said to get the work done was, "Do what is lawful," reminding the novice to act according to the cultural tenet, not ordering him.

This last illustration introduces a further principle: that of structure. Many people in our society have been apprehensive of the implications of personal autonomy, because they have felt that it is apt to lead to lawlessness and chaos. Yet actually it is in connection with the highest personal autonomy that we often find the most intricately developed structure; and it is this structure that makes autonomy possible in a group situation. For example, the Burmese novices could proceed without receiving orders only because the structure clearly indicated what could and could not be done and at what time of the day or month or year.

Margaret Mead and Gregory Bateson have described this combination of autonomy and structure for the Balinese. These people have an exceedingly complex calendrical system, consisting of a permutation of ten weeks of differing lengths; and this system, in combination with an intricately patterned spacial and status system, furnishes the structure according to which an individual behaves. For instance, according to the specific combinaton of "weeks" on which his birthday falls, and according to his status, an individual has to participate in a special way at a particular temple festival. No one imposes this tribute upon him; and no one asks for his contribution. However, because of the enormous amount of detail involved in the precision of the structure, there are officials known as reminders, who merely remind the people of the exact character of the pending festival. Each person then proceeds to act according to his peculiar position in the temporal structure, acting autonomously, finding guidance in the structure.

When the specific aspects of the structure are not clear, the people in such societies can turn to authority for clarification. And here we often find, as with the Burmese or the Navaho Indians, that the authority of the headman or the chief or the leader is in many ways like the authority of the dictionary, or of Einstein. There is no hint of coercion or command here; the people go to the leader with faith, as we go to a reference book, and the leader answers according to his greater knowledge, or clarifies an obscure point, or amplifies according to his greater experience and wisdom. He does not say: You must do this, because I order you to. Yet, he does use the *must* or its equivalent; he says, so to speak: As I see it, this is what must be done. In a sense, it is like the recipe which says: You must not open the oven door for ten minutes after you put the cake in. No housewife, preparing a cake and going to the cookbook for guidance, feels that her personal integrity is violated by this interdiction.

Once she is committed to the cake-making, she finds the recipe, the structure, enabling and guiding; she finds it freeing, not restricting.

If permissiveness at times leads to lawlessness and chaos, and even to immobilization instead of the freedom to be and to act, this happens usually in those cases where "permission" goes from person to person, in a structural vacuum. It happens when the structure is by-passed through the dictatorial permissiveness of the person who takes it upon himself to allow, and by implication to forbid, another person. In the societies which were mentioned above, where we find absolute valuing of unique being, what often takes the form of permissiveness in our society exists as the freedom to be, and to find actualization; and it is found within a clearly delineated structure.

Such is the society of the Navaho Indians of Arizona and New Mexico. How long this picture will last, we cannot predict. The mineral resources of their land are now being developed, and rapid change is being introduced. What I say here draws on the autobiographies of Navaho men, as well as on recent ethnographies.

In these accounts, we find a tightly knit group, depending on mutual responsibility among all its members, a precisely structured universe, and a great respect for individual autonomy and integrity. We find people who maintain an inviolable privacy while living as a family in a one-room house, sharing work and responsibility to such an extent that even a child of six will contribute his share of mutton to the family meal. The family unit is so closely knit that, if a child of five is ill or absent, the family suffers because there is a gap in the cooperative effort; and when a man goes hunting, he can get nothing unless his wife cooperates at home by observing the necessary taboos. The well-being of a Navaho, his health and the health of all his undertakings, depend on the maintenance of harmony with nature. All being is both good and evil; and by walking carefully according to a highly structured map of procedure, within a detailed framework of "do's" and "don'ts," the Navaho can keep the proper balance of good and evil in his life, and thus find health and harmony. The rules according to which he lives originate in the structure, and come to him as guidance from the parents, not as commands.

Within this structured universe and tightly knit society, the Navaho lives in personal autonomy. Adults and children are valued for their sheer being, just because they *are*. There is no urge toward achievement; no one has to strive for success. In fact, neither is there reward for success, nor is success held out as a reward for hard work. Wealth may be the result of hard work and skill, but obviously it is also the blatant result of lack of generosity, lack of responsibility for one's relatives, perhaps even of malicious witchcraft. No good Navaho becomes and remains "wealthy" in our terms.

Hard work is valued in itself, as a personal quality which combines the ability to withstand hardship with the paramount sense of responsibility for the work of the group. Even a young child will be trained to see to it that the whole flock of sheep is safe before he takes shelter during a blizzard. This means a systematic program in developing hardihood. He is waked up at daybreak in winter, so that he may run for miles; and in summer, he runs in the hot sun of noontime. Presently, he intensifies this program by his own decision, perhaps putting sand in his moccasins to make the running more rigorous; that is, he relates himself to this discipline with spontaneity. Children learn responsibility by being given indispensable household tasks; in addition, they are given sheep of their own from the time they are about five. They are responsible for the care and welfare of these animals; thus, they acquire a further opportunity at responsible participation. Now they can take their turn at supplying the meat for the family meal, and they can contribute mutton when this is needed for ceremonials, or to entertain visitors.

Most of all, an individual has to learn to walk safely through life, maintaining his harmony with the universe. This involves learning to observe a large number of taboos and procedures, which are aspects of every act: to learn, for example, what is to be done with the left hand, which direction to have his hogan face, what is to be started in a sunwise direction, or to be taken from the east side of a tree; what to avoid touching, or saying, or looking at. All this could be seen as inhibiting, or negative, or as interfering with the individual; but to the Navaho it is guidance in the acquisition of an essential skill—the freedom to act and to be. The intricate set of regulations is like a map which affords freedom to proceed to a man lost in the jungle.

In Navaho autobiographies we often find the phrase, "I followed the advice of my parents," but rarely, "I obeyed my parents." The good Navaho does not command his child; and a mother who is aggressive toward her children, who "talks rough" to them, is strongly criticized. In teaching her children the tremendous number of taboos they have to learn for their well-being, the good Navaho mother does not say: I will punish you if you do thus-and-thus; but: Such-and-such an unpleasant thing will happen to you. The mother is guiding the child; and if the child takes a wrong turn, if he breaks a taboo, he is not "guilty." He has not committed a sin against the mother and is not in need of forgiveness. He has made a mistake which he must set right.

This attitude is basic to all Navaho relatedness, so that here man is not burdened with guilt, and does not feel apologetic toward human or divine beings. He is neither grateful nor abject to his gods. As a matter of fact, he must never humble himself before them, since the process of healing, of the recovery of harmony with the universe, involves identification with the appropriate god, who would be slighted if the patient humiliated himself. This means that the Navaho has—and indeed must have—as much respect and value for himself as for others; in fact, this is the Navaho version of the principle that we have discovered so recently in our society: that we cannot accept and respect others until we learn to accept and respect ourselves.

In what I have said, I have made no distinction between adults and children, as the Navaho do not differentiate between the two in the respect they show for personal autonomy. There is no minority status for children. For example, a good Navaho will not take it upon himself to speak for another, whether for adult or child. A man, asked by a White what his wife thinks on a certain subject, is likely to answer, "I don't know, I haven't asked her." In the same way, a father, asked to sell his child's bow and arrow, will refer the request to a five-year-old boy, and abide by the child's decision not to sell, even though he knows the child is badly in need of the clothing that can be bought with the price of the toy. A woman, asked whether a certain baby could talk, said "Yes"; and when the ethnographer was puzzled by the "meaningless" sounds the baby was making, she explained that the baby could talk, but she could not understand what the baby said. All that she had the right to do was to speak for herself, to say that she could not understand. She would not presume to speak for the child, and to say—as I think we would have said—that the child was making meaningless sounds.

So the individual remains inviolate. No one coerces another among the Navaho. Traditionally, parents do not force their children to do what they unequivocally do not want to do, such as going to school or to the hospital; children are not coerced even "for their own good." As the mother of two unschooled children put it, "I listen to my children, and I have to take their word." There is no political coercion, and all leadership is traditionally incidental. A man finds himself in a position of leadership when the people seek him out because of the high degree of his inner development; because of his wisdom, his knowledge, his assumption of responsibility, his physical skill and hardihood, the wealth which he is ready to use to help his relatives. Men do not seek leadership; and White employers have found that the Navaho are reluctant to become foremen, however able they may be, and in spite of the higher pay involved. It is "fundamentally indecent" according to Clyde Kluckhohn, "for a single individual to presume to make decisions for the group," and therefore not even a leader will make decisions for others, or give orders to others.

For the Navaho mother, personal autonomy means that her child has the freedom to make his own mistakes, to suffer pain or grief or joy and learn from experience. And the child has his freedom because the mother has faith in him. This does not mean that she has high expectations of him, but that she trusts him. She knows that he is a mingling of good and evil; she knows that life is unpredictable, and that a mistake may bring disaster. But she is willing to refrain from interfering with her child as he explores, as he takes his steps in life. When the baby starts walking, the mother does not see to it that he is out of reach of the fire, and that all the sharp knives have been put away. The child gets burned a little, and the mother helps him learn from this experience that he has to be careful of fire; he has a small accident, and the mother helps him understand and deal with that particular danger. By taking a chance on her child, the mother teaches him to be ready to meet and deal with danger, instead of warning him away from danger.

This trust means that the child has freedom to move, to act, to undertake responsibility. It means that the child is given significant tasks in the household. A psychiatrist visiting a Navaho family wrote in her diary: "After supper the girl (ten years old) went to water the horses, and the boy (five years old) to take the little flock back to some older members of the family who lived in a hogan a quarter of a mile away." No mention is made here of orders given, nor of any checking on the mother's part to see that the job was done.

Coexistence of Autonomy and Limits

If the societies I have mentioned here present an enviable consistency in the expression of the principle of individual integrity, it is well to keep in mind that there may be no special virtue in this; at the time these societies were studied, they enjoyed great social homogeneity, and were relatively unchanging over time. This means that the children could learn the adult role at home by gradually sharing the life of the father or mother

—as a matter of course, expecting and wanting to live the life of the parents, and to hold the same values and principles. However, the fact remains that consistency was there; that the principle was upheld by the various aspects of the culture, even by the very grammar of the language, as among the Wintu.

The practices I have presented here are not for us to copy, but rather food for thought, the basis for new insights. I have tried to show that law and limits and personal autonomy can coexist effectively, that spontaneity is not necessarily killed by group responsibility, that respect for individual integrity is not an end to be achieved by specific means, but that it can exist only if it is supported by deep conviction and by the entire way of life.

REFERENCES

Dyk, Walter, Recorder. Son of Old Man Hat. A Navaho Autobiography. New York: Harcourt, Brace and Company, 1938.

Kluckhohn, Clyde and Dorothea Leighton. The Navaho. Cambridge: Harvard University Press, 1946.

Leighton, Dorothea and Clyde Kluckhohn. Children of the People. Cambridge: Harvard University Press, 1947.

Reichard, Gladys A. Prayer, The Compulsive Word. Monographs of the American Ethnological Society. J. J. Augustin, New York, 1944.

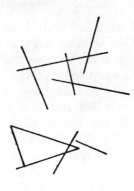

Personal Significance
and Group Structure

I HAVE WRITTEN THIS PAPER IN RE-
sponse to a request to present a dilemma in my family life, and describe
the compromise through which I solved it. But when I began speaking of
such a situation in my family, I realized that it was not a dilemma but
rather what I would call a problematic situation. When I looked at it, I
saw that there was one way that I simply could not go, and another way
that was the only way I could go. It was not a question of weighing alternatives, and certainly not one of making a compromise. When I pursued
it to its basic issues, I found that I had to choose between personal growth
and autonomy for my children on the one hand, the submersion of the
self in the group on the other; and to me the choice was clear.

A factor in the situation which confronted me came from my own
personal history. I am of Greek origin. I came to this country as a foreign
student, eventually married an American, and I am now bringing up four
children in this country with full rights to the heritage of its culture. I am
constantly aware of the fact that the only upbringing I have experienced
immediately is Greek, whereas I am bringing up four American citizens
who must feel American, think American, and relate themselves in an
American way, not a Greek way.

Personal Significance . . . From *Integrity and Compromise: Problems of Public and
Private Conscience*, Religion and Civilization Series, Harper & Brothers, New York, 1957.

My husband and I raised our children according to principles which we shared. One of these was that the self should never be conceived as an isolate, nor as the focus of the universe, but rather that it should be defined as a social self. We valued society. We believed that only through society could the self grow, be enriched, find strength. We strongly believed in what MacIver calls "community"—in the "Gemeinschaft." However, we became increasingly aware of the fact that our children were individuals, that they liked to make their own choices and decisions. They did not like to conform to the standards of a group, and in fact they did not enjoy groups. They did not seek out gangs of children of their own age. They did not classify according to age; they liked "people," and referred to other children as "people." They enjoyed groups only when these were based on individual friendships binding person to person. They preferred to choose one or two friends, and to develop a deep and growing relationship.

The one group which they completely enjoyed, in which they were completely involved, was the family. But it was not a group to them; it just happened to them; it was not a group they went out to join, but one that just grew. They had taken no steps to create such a group. Within the family they did not seem to seek individual independent behavior or choice which went counter to the ends of the family. But when it came to joining organizations such as the Scouts, they all turned away. And this reluctance to see meaning in organized groups with a group purpose seemed completely un-American.

I did not worry about this while my husband, who came from generations of Americans, was with me to carry the burden of making the children into good Americans. But when I was left to bring up the children alone, I felt the need to go against the family-centered upbringing of my Greek culture, so as to "socialize" my children in the American way. I was afraid that, falling between two stools, my children would grow into isolated individuals, cut off from all social nourishment. And I believed in society, as a person and as an anthropologist. Among the primitive societies I had studied, I found people who were rich in human quality, poised, strong, true, unique, people who grew from birth until death. These were people who had social selves, who lived in societies where individual ends and social ends coincided.

While I was considering this problem, I was offered an opportunity to move to a Middle West city where there was much concern over group development and group participation; where group awareness and participation was being implemented at all levels in the schools. This transfer seemed to offer the solution I was looking for. We moved. The children were unhappy at school, but I tried to help them to acquiesce to the new system, to understand its principles, to adjust to a group-centered environment. But, since my working hours coincided with school hours, I had no direct experience of what went on until the Parents' Open Night before Thanksgiving.

I went first of all to my son's room, the seventh grade. The teacher showed me a mural, covering all the walls, depicting the life of the ancient Egyptians. It was a group project, and the teacher pointed out the part for which my son was responsible. The painting depicted a war scene: some pinkish, sleek, placid, fat, lifeless horses. These were nothing like the horses I had seen my son draw at previous times—skinny, elongated beasts, full of straining movement and savage life. I protested that these lifeless horses could not be my son's doing. The teacher explained that my son had not been allowed to paint his own unique horses; they were too different. Since this was a group project, uniformity was essential, so the children had all copied illustrations from a history textbook. As I turned away, appalled and only half-convinced, I spotted the tiny figure of a bird, of no known genus, scraggy, leering, menacing, and I knew that my son's uniqueness had not been entirely mowed down in the drive for uniformity; it had burst through, however irrelevantly and illicitly. It reminded me of the mushrooms which push up a cement pavement, cracking and disrupting its even surface. I was happy to see it.

Disturbed at this interpretation of the concept of the group, I went to the classroom of my daughter who was in the fourth grade. The teacher pointed to a frieze of Pilgrims and Indians in profile that ran around the wall of the room, and obviously waited for my admiring response. All the Pilgrims were alike, all the Indians alike without deviation; alike in size and shape and color. I did not know what I was expected to admire, and finally asked whether the children had pasted up the frieze. The teacher explained that they not only had pasted it, they had actually made it, as a group project. "It was hard to make all the heads alike," she said. "When the children first painted the pictures they all looked different, so we had to throw them away. And then I made an Indian profile and a Pilgrim profile; I wrote directions for coloring each part, and the children traced them and cut out their own. And now they make *one* frieze."

I had another daughter in the tenth grade in high school; and soon after this sad night, her grade decided to have a bake sale to help raise money for a trip to Washington in their senior year. This did seem like good group participation. The trip was to be a truly cooperative venture, since all the students in the class were working toward it, though not all would manage to go eventually. This time each student was asked to bring cake or cookies for the sale.

My daughter Mary took the bake sale seriously, and was using it as a learning opportunity. She stayed up late making four batches of cookies for which I contributed the ingredients. She found out the cost of the ingredients, and priced the cookies, adding an appropriate amount for her skilled labor. When she took them to school, she discovered that this was not what had been expected of her. Half the children had asked their mothers to bake for them, and most of the rest had bought baked goods at the corner bakery. Mary's cookies were priced below the cost of the raw materials, as were all the other goods, to make sure that they would sell; yet the students were congratulated on raising all this money for their trip through their own exertions.

Mary, concerned over what seemed hypocrisy, decided that the work of the students in selling the cookies would represent their involvement, their share in the raising of funds. But when the time came for the sale, the homeroom teacher was there to sell. The teenagers could not be trusted to make change. True, they were studying geometry, but they might make a mistake in subtraction; and besides they might yield to temptation. The group could not expose itself to the fallibility of its members; it could not take a chance on the integrity or the ability of its constituent members. In the interest of ensuring good results for the group project, all the strivings of the individual self had to be suppressed, while the homeroom teacher handled the project.

This is what I found in my children's schools. Was this the end of my search for true group experience? Was this the meaning of the self in society? I saw here not nourishment and enrichment, but impoverishment and diminution of the self. The group here demanded the sacrifice of the very generative force of the self, the vitality, the vagary, the spontaneity. It was superimposed upon the self as an external standard, and could be sustained only through a Procrustean conformity. In these schools the children were not people; not individual persons with integrity peculiar to each. Their being did not call forth respect. What was demanded of them was to form a class based on undeviating similarity; and to achieve this, the striving of the self had to be throttled. Only through destruction of the self could the group thrive.

I was not convinced that this was necessary to the creation of a group. In my study of other people, I had come across societies where the group was far more permeating in the life of the individual, yet where even the private thoughts and feelings of individuals affected the group. I had studied the Hopi where, within a strong group structure, each person had unique significance; where the people were spontaneous, vital, free, strong. So I went back to a consideration of the Hopi, to find out what there was about their culture which made it possible for an individual to maintain uniqueness and significance within the group structure.

Whatever I say here about the Hopi refers to them as they have been until recently. Change has been going on, and particularly since the past war, when many Hopi went out, either with the armed forces, or to factories, and became more and more exposed to our ways of arranging things, to our way of life. If I use what seems to be the present tense, I use it in its reference to the timeless: to what they call the Hopi way—the good, the right path; not necessarily to how they live, but to the good life. Only when I give specific examples do I speak of individual Hopi, of the actual events of time and space. At this time, there are only two villages where the traditional Hopi way is maintained.

The Hopi are Pueblo Indians, living in Arizona. They reckon descent through the mother, and houses belong to the women of the lineage, where their husbands come to join them. In the older villages, the closely related women—sisters, mothers and daughters, aunts and cousins —with their families, occupy one or more adjacent households, where the work of living goes on cooperatively. The men herd, farm, hunt, collect fuel, perhaps spin and weave; the women cooperate in preparing food for the group, caring for young children and for the house, hauling water, making pottery and baskets. And when I say men and women I include boys and girls, who from an early age have the right to work alongside the adults, doing work important to the welfare of the group.

The group, starting from the unit of the immediate family of birth, but expanding through systematic introduction into wider areas until it includes eventually the entire universe, is the focus to which the behavior and feeling and entire being of an individual is oriented. Much, if not all, of what a person thinks and does, has a reference to the group. For example, if I go visiting a new mother in my society, I shall probably smile with the joy of seeing her again, with congratulations for her new baby. The Hopi visitor will smile also, but here the smile has a significance beyond this, as the happiness it expresses helps the baby to thrive and the new mother to recover her strength; and, conversely, a face expressing worry would bring harm at this time.

A person enters the unit by birth, and all of an individual's behavior is geared to this social unit which he has joined through no choice of his own. His loyalties are to this group; they are not person-to-person loyalties. And parents have been known deliberately to try to shift a child's affection from concentration upon one family member, to diffusion among the group. The area of an individual's work, of responsible participation, is therefore not one he has chosen, but is given also, as it is coextensive with the group. Every individual, young and old, is charged with responsibility for the welfare of the social unit; and this they apparently accept voluntarily, considering it good.

Richard Brandt, a philosopher making a study of Hopi ethics, found that his informants considered that one of the main things which make a man ashamed was that of not having any children alive. This "shows sin"; that is, it shows that a man's behavior, his thoughts, his willing, his emotions were not social enough to keep his children alive. People were expected to be ashamed of not helping in cooperative undertakings, not giving, not participating in ceremonials for the welfare of the unit—in this last case, the entire universe. No, said the informants, a man need not be ashamed of being poor, or of being dumb, so long as he was good to others. Brandt made arrangements to see informants in absolute secrecy, to protect them against possible criticism; but even so, he found that the informant might not be ready to talk until he had made sure that no harm would come to the group from his disclosures.

Related to this is the Hopi reluctance to stand out, to be singled out from the group. Teachers in Hopi schools have reported discomfort and even tears as a reaction to praise in public. It appears that what is in fact disturbing is the comparative evaluation that results in singling out and praising. Hopi do not compare their achievement, nor the importance of their work, and "a highly skilled stone-cutter is perfectly content to accept the same wages as an unskilled day laborer." Children cannot be persuaded to compete in school, in classwork or in playing games. One school reported that the children learned to play basketball easily, and delighted in the game; but they could not be taught to keep score. They played by the hour, without knowing who was winning. Without emphasis on the score, the structure of the game, with everyone doing his utmost within his established role, is in a simplified way similar to the kind of structure we find in the Hopi group.

As I have indicated earlier, it is not only the physical act, or overt behavior, which is effective, according to the Hopi view. Thought and will and intent are at least as effective; so that it is not enough for the individual to act peacefully; he must also feel nonaggressive, think harmonious thoughts, and be imbued with a singleness of purpose. It is his duty to be happy, for the sake of the group, and a mind in conflict and full of anxiety brings disruption, ill-being, to the social unit, and, at a time of prayer and ceremonial, to the entire universe.

Brandt found that one of the personal traits highly valued was that of being "happy in his heart." One informant told him, "This is like a flower or a cornfield: when in bloom it beautifies the whole earth . . . It is a kind of gratitude. . . . When you go into the fields you should sing to the corn." Another informant praised a man who, even when upset, made "himself happy while talking" with others. Superficially, this is similar to valued behavior in our own society, too; but with the Hopi, it is an aspect of working for the group.

Human society is a part of a larger structured whole, so an individual cooperates with even more than the members of his human group. Every aspect of nature, plants and rocks and animals, colors and cardinal directions and numbers and sex distinctions, the dead and the living, all have a cooperative share in the maintenance of the universal order. Eventually, the effort of each individual, human or not, goes into this huge whole. And here, too, it is every aspect of a person which counts. The entire being of the Hopi individual affects the balance of nature; and as each individual develops his inner potential, as he enhances his participation, so does the entire universe become invigorated. Not his behavior alone, not his achievement, but his entire unique being is significant.

Much of the time and energy of the Hopi goes into working at ceremonials. These are highly organized and form part of an established ceremonial cycle. Each ceremony "belongs to" a secret society, usually a men's society and only members of this society have the privilege and the responsibility of carrying out the ceremony. Each main ceremony involves an exceedingly complex order of detailed acts; preparatory rites, acts of purification, gathering of materials, preparation of masks and sand paintings and medicine water, composition of new songs, rehearsal of dances. The women prepare food to be exchanged reciprocally. The ceremonials themselves last nine or seventeen days. Though only one secret society is charged with the responsibility of a specific ceremony, the entire group of "spectators"—all the villagers and visitors from other pueblos who come to the public performances—eventually participate, through keeping a "good heart," through their wholehearted involvement in what they watch, through laughing at the burlesque and pranks afforded by the clowns.

Each main ceremony has reference to a phase of the agricultural cycle, helping the universal order to become actual. There is an established course for the sun, for example, within the cosmic order; but the winter solstice ceremony is necessary to actualize this order into the here and now, so that the sun can actually follow the prescribed course, and so turn northward. The growing of the corn also has its established order; the stages of growth are given in the order of nature; but the corn cannot move through them, from germination to fruition, without the cooperative effort of man, who must transform, by means of his ceremonials, potentiality into actuality. So, in the end, when a field of corn is ready to harvest, it is a result of the cooperative effort of every member of the group, in addition to the man who has dug and hoed and planted and weeded.

Though each ceremonial has specific reference within the agricultural cycle, each main ceremony also has reference to the whole of life, to the entire cosmic system. The aim is the well-being of the universal whole, not of the individual. If the individual profits by the ceremonial, it is because he is an integral part of this whole which has become invigorated. The individual maintains harmony with the universe for the sake of the universal order, and only derivatively for his own sake. Eventually, through the maintenance of this harmony, the human group thrives, the sun moves along its established course from solstice to solstice, the thunderclouds gather and release their rain, the corn sprouts and roots and fills and ripens.

In all this, the individual is working along given lines, for given ends, for a group which he did not create of his own choice. This seems the denial of all freedom and initiative.

In addition, the geographic location of the Hopi seems to make for determinism, and an absence of individual freedom. They live and practice agriculture in country where it would seem at first glance to be impossible to depend on the land for a living. The rain may not come at all, or may fall in torrents and wash away the crops; high winds may blow away the seed. The growing cycle of corn, the main crop, is almost coincidental with the growing season, which is cut short at both ends by killing frosts. As Laura Thompson says: "The arid north Arizona plateau posed unyielding imperatives which had to be met habitually and unerringly if the tribe were to survive and reproduce itself. . . ." This means that the environment imposes rigid limits to behavior and choice. How can man have personal freedom to will, to act, to be, in these circumstances when the very environment dictates behavior, and where there is so little margin for human fallibility? Where can there be room for personal initiative? Who can be proud of bringing his stand of corn to fruition when even the laughter of a child has gone to grow it? How can there be motivation for work, when the responsibility and the results and the work itself are all shared, to a greater or less extent? Does not this mean that personal effort is lost in the undifferentiated immensity, that the individual is submerged and lost in the group and in the universal whole?

The genius of his culture has made it possible for the Hopi to find spontaneity, significance and freedom, motivation and personal integrity within this structured universe, within the given society, and the difficult environment. It is true that there is probably no joy of independent achievement, but this does not mean that there is no motivation, no personal initiative.

Certainly, there is no such thing as individualism, in our sense of the term. There is no private enterprise; there is avoidance of outstandingness. There is no undertaking which an individual initiates and brings to a conclusion alone, with the pride of success. When a farmer is harvesting a "successful" corn crop, who has "succeeded"? Throughout the year, the members of his pueblo, in different organizations, have performed an established series of ceremonies to bring about this harvest. The children have played organized ball games for days with the children from another pueblo, and thus helped the corn to grow. Men have refrained from intercourse with their wives, and sweethearts; eaglets have been captured at considerable risk, women and children have laughed heartily at the antics of ceremonial clowns, priests have gone into retirement and meditation, and much more has been done and wished and thought, to bring about this good harvest. The farmer's achievement in all this may be seen as insignificant; yet it may also be seen as superbly significant.

For the immensity of effort is not undifferentiated; the individual effort is not like a grain of sand, lost in the universal whole. Every individual within the system has his unique role,[1] and each role is different and indispensable. The structured whole of the universe, or of the human group, contains a precise position for each and every member. No one is expendable. In Laura Thompson's words, "Every individual in the group, male and female, young or old, has his proper place and role in the organization of the community . . . with duties and rights commensurate with their age and status." And, in the universal whole, every part of nature has its unique and indispensable role. Man supplies the moving principle in this order through his ability to will, and through his ceremonials.

So each individual person, through the uniqueness of his role and the

---

[1] By "role" I mean a specific place in the structural whole, which carries with it responsible, non-interchangeable function.

indispensability of his own specific effort, has great significance. Group effort and community of ends does not mean totalitarianism and the loss of individual uniqueness. In fact, the group can prosper only to the extent that this uniqueness is fully actualized. Only in so far as each member of each *kiva* carries out his own unique responsibility, fulfills his role in putting on and performing the ceremony which is the responsibility of this particular ceremonial association, will the ceremony help the corn to move into the next stage of growth. In this each individual member has an indispensable and precise function.

The clarity of role, the preciseness of structure and of place in the structure is such that the individual knows what is open to him to do; and, as it is apparently satisfying to work in terms of the social unit, the individual can and does work autonomously within his role. O'Kane writes, "A Hopi household is a self-directing group, the members of which seem to achieve automatic coordination of their activities. No one tells the others what they should do, or when, or how. No one exercises authority. The various members seem to fall naturally into a pattern in which the abilities of the individual and the needs of the household are satisfactorily served. . . ."

Thus an individual can decide to what extent he will fill the responsibility which is his privilege. For example, O'Kane tells how three fellow clansmen decided to get turtles to supply themselves with shell for the leg rattles used in ceremonial dancing. This was done at their own initiative, but within an established framework—that is, the rattles were to be attached to a specified part of the leg, they were to be of specified shell, worn at specified times in specified roles, and so forth. The individual decision brought more shell rattles, or newer rattles to the *kivas* involved; it enriched the group. The decision involved much arduous work, including a return journey of some six hundred miles. Each of the three contributed of what he had to offer—one his car, another gas, the third his knowledge and skill. There was no attempt at uniformity, nor at equalization; there was no suppression of individuality; rather through the variety of individual contribution, the whole could be achieved.

The individual is free to choose ways in which to actualize his responsibility; as, for example, when three children, whose grandmother was dying in their home, asked to stay after school because they were afraid that they could not avoid anxious thoughts if they went back to the pueblo. The projective tests reported by Thompson and Joseph show that for Hopi children responsible group participation is often named a happy experience.

It is clear that the welfare of the group and of the entire universe eventually depends on the individual; yet the individual is neither tethered, nor monitored, nor shackled, nor coerced, to insure his safe carrying out of his responsibilities. When Brandt was asking questions involving ethical principles, he found that there was no adherence to group morals as categorical. "It is up to him to decide what is right or wrong," the individual stated repeatedly, and the desirability of consent was stressed: "I don't believe in forcing anybody to do anything. . . . If he gives his consent, it is all right."

It is evident, then, that a tremendous respect and trust is accorded to the individual since no provision is made for a man's failure, neglect, error. The entire group and the entire universe is vulnerable, exposed to the fallibility of the individual. Even a child, allowing himself to have anxious thoughts, can bring ill to the pueblo. This means a great responsibility, and can be seen as a frightening and overwhelming burden. Yet, instead of blocking the individual with its immensity, this responsibility seems to function as a motivating factor, affording a channel for spontaneity. Instead of cutting off the protruding variations, the idiosyncrasies of the individual; instead of submerging the self within a uniform mass, the group encourages individual quality, and enriches itself through it. The significant place given to each person and the full trust accorded to each means that the group thrives only through the full exercise of the individual self.

This is what I had missed in the school situation of my children; I had missed significance and respect for unique being. There was no trust in the potentiality of each child, of *this* child. The homeroom protected itself against its members; it would not take a chance on the honesty or mathematical ability or industry of its members. The person had no individual worth; and, in fact, effort was directed toward making the members of the group interchangeable, until the artistic expression of one could not be distinguished from that of another. There was no appreciation of difference; it was treated as disruptive and threatening to group welfare; and, being cast into the outer darkness, it did, in fact, disrupt. If my son had drawn the Egyptian war scene in his own peculiar lines, he would have had no occasion to introduce his minute discordant bird in the corner. Some growth of the self did occur, because of its tremendous impetus; but it met with discouragement. I found here that the group existed at the expense of the individual; and this was totalitarianism.

At this point my problem was clear and I solved it. What did I do? I decided that I needed a school where the group was conceived according to democratic principles; where the individual was given a significant place within the structured group; where the group was considered to prosper only through the optimum growth of each and every member—not through the stunting of any one; where uniqueness was valued; where individual and group could grow and thrive only together. I found such a school and moved to that town, fifty miles away. I solved my problem. My children are growing up in true American democracy.

REFERENCES

Brandt, Richard B. *Hopi Ethics: A Theoretical Analysis.* Chicago: University of Chicago Press, 1954.

O'Kane, Walter Collins. *The Hopis: Portrait of a Desert People.* Norman: University of Oklahoma Press, 1953.

Simmons, Leo W. *Sun Chief.* New Haven: Yale University Press, 1942.

Stephen, Alexander M. *Hopi Journal.* E. C. Parsons (ed.) New York: Columbia University Press, 1936.

Thompson, Laura. *Culture in Crisis: A Study of the Hopi Indians.* New York: Harper & Brothers, 1950.

Thompson, Laura and Alice Joseph. *The Hopi Way.* Chicago: University of Chicago Press, 1944.

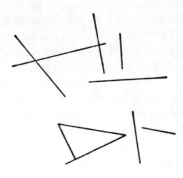

The Joy of Work

as Participation

IT WAS IN A DOMESTIC SITUATION THAT I had that moment of discovery of which I want to write now. It was Christmas Eve; I was working late at night, listening to the desultory talk of my husband and my brother-in-law. I was exhausted after a day of housework, of coping with two small children, of Christmas preparations; but I had to finish making bedding for a doll crib, and I was working against time, wishing I were in bed.

I had been living a life of conflict since my marriage, since I had felt that I owed it to my profession to continue my work in anthropology. This meant that I had to organize my life so that my housewifely duties did not encroach unduly on my professional work; and I had to justify everything that I did as a housewife, as something imposed by the exigencies of my budget or by my role as wife and mother. In this way, I did not have to feel guilty toward my profession. The doll blanket I was making that night was amply justified; it would give happiness to my three-year-old daughter, and it had been necessary for me to take the time to make crib and bedding, for I could not afford to buy them.

From *The Hour of Insight: A Sequel to Moments of Personal Discovery*. Religion and Civilization Series, Harper & Brothers, New York, 1953.

As I sewed this Christmas Eve, I was suddenly astonished to discover that I had started to add an entirely unpremeditated and unnecessary edging of embroidery; and, simultaneously, I was aware of a deep enjoyment in what I was doing. It was a feeling that had nothing to do with the pleasure the work would give to my daughter on the morrow; it had nothing to do with a sense of achievement, or of virtue in duty accomplished. And I knew that I had never liked to embroider. There was no justification for my work; yet it was the source of such a deep satisfaction, that the late hour and my fatigue had ceased to exist for me.

At this moment of discovery, I knew that I was experiencing what it meant to be a social being, not merely Dorothy Lee, an individual; I knew that I had truly become a mother, a wife, a neighbor, a teacher. I realized that some boundary had disappeared, so that I was working in a social medium; that I was not working for the future pleasure of a distant daughter, but rather within a relationship unaffected by temporality or physical absence. What gave meaning to my work was the medium in which I was working—the medium of love, in a broad sense. So far, my rationalization and justification of my work had obscured this meaning, had cut me off from my own social context. It suddenly became clear to me that it did not matter whether I was scrubbing the kitchen floor or darning stockings or zipping up snowsuits; these all had meaning, not in themselves, but in terms of the situation of which they were a part. They contained social value because they implemented the value of the social situation.

This was a tremendous discovery for me, illuminating in a flash my experience and my thinking. My mind went immediately to the Tikopia, about whom I had been reading, and I said to myself, "This is the way the Tikopia work." I had been puzzled about the motivating forces in the life of the Tikopia. These were people who were without organized leadership in work, yet who carried out large undertakings. And without any authority to impose legislation and mete out punishment, the business of the village was carried out, and law and order were maintained. Raymond Firth, the ethnographer, answering the unspoken questions of western readers, spoke of obligations, duty, fear of adverse opinion, as motivations. I did not like his choice of words, because he spoke of the obligation to perform unpleasant tasks, for example, and yet the situations he described brimmed with joy. Now I saw that the Tikopia did not need external incentives.

This was all very well, but when I came to examine my discovery, I could not explain it in any rational or acceptable way. My society did not structure working situations as occasions which contained their own satisfaction; and it assumed the existence of aggregates or collections of individuals, not of a social continuum. I had learned to believe in the existence of a distinct self, relating itself externally to work as a means to an end, with external incentives and external rewards. Yet it was obvious that if I got satisfaction from participating in a situation, there must be some medium, some continuum, within which this participation can take place. If my family and I were aspects of one whole, there must be some positive apprehension of a continuity which made me an aspect of my family, not a separate member; it was not enough to say that my physical being and my sensory experience did not in themselves prescribe the limits of the self.

And this is how I came to study the definition of the self among the Tikopia. It seemed to me that only on the basis of just such an assumption of continuity could their relations to man and nature and the divine, their words and phrasings and ceremonials be understood. I went back to Raymond Firth's books on the Tikopia, and read each detail without placing it automatically against my own conception of the self. And so I was able to see a conception of identity radically different from mine; I found a social definition of the self. I found that here I could not speak of man's relations with his universe, but rather of a universal interrelatedness, because man was not the focus from which relations flowed. I found a named and recognized medium of social continuity, implemented in social acts, not in words. And I found, for example, that an act of fondling or an embrace was not phrased as a "demonstration" or an "expression" of affection—that is, starting from the ego and defined in terms of the emotions of the ego, but rather as an act of moral support or of comforting or of sharing, as a social act. I found a system of childrearing which trained toward increasing interdependence and socialization, instead of toward personal self-reliance and individuation. And here I found work whose motivation lay in the situation itself, a situation which included the worker and his society, the activity and its end, and whose satisfaction lay in social value.

What I say below is based on three books by Raymond Firth, *We the Tikopia, Primitive Polynesian Economy,* and *The Work of the Gods,* parts I and II. The interpretation is usually my own, based on intensive and detailed reading of this rich source of data.

In Firth's presentation, the newborn Tikopia is not helped to recognize, discover, develop—or is it create?—his own separate identity; in fact, he is not treated as if he had such a separate identity. In my own culture, I had learned to speak of an infant as an "addition" to the family; and my planning for the coming baby had been in terms of something added. I found an additional room, additional furniture, and added implements; I took out an additional insurance policy. But Firth spoke as if the child were no such addition. He spoke of the "entrance" of the child into a family circle, and everything he subsequently described conveyed the impression of a swelling of this circle, of an enhancement of social participation and social good.

From birth on, among the Tikopia, the infant is gradually and systematically introduced to a widening circle. At first, he is physically close to his mother, held and suckled and comforted when awake, in immediate tactile contact. Soon the female aunts and other older relatives share this close care of, or involvement in, the infant. Then the father and the older male relatives begin to nurse the child, seeking his companionship. More and more distant relatives come, male and female; and the child is introduced to their society deliberately, so that his affection and dependence should be spread widely. At some point during this process, the child is also introduced to the companionship of youths and maidens and little children. The infant may be turned over to the care of a six-year-old brother, who will be seen carrying him around, nuzzling and playing with him, and otherwise showing his enjoyment of him. Adolescent boys and girls, exchanging flirtatious talk in the shade, may choose to hold an infant in their arms.

This is not merely a recognition of the dependence of the infant. It is an expression of the interdependence within the social unit. Close and distant relatives leave their homes and their occupations to be with a little grandchild or niece or cousin several times removed; or to carry a young relative off for a visit, or down to the beach where the men sit together talking. It is not for lack of babysitters that babies are taken along by their parents when they go gardening. Firth speaks of how a man, called away from talk of men by his wife to stay with the baby, leaves the group with a sense of dignity, not of annoyance and interruption.

Many Tikopia parents go even further in widening the circle in which their children participate. They lend them out as "adhering" children to other households; then the children are parts of two family circles, sharing the intimate details of living with either, at their choice. Older children or adults may be invited to become adhering brothers or sisters or other relatives.

The structure of life within the family rests on the assumption that there is social continuity, and that this is good. In our own society, where we assume individual identity, we keep the physical entities strictly separate; only in sexual relations do we allow physical mingling. We do not like to breathe the breath of others, or feel the breath of others; and, evoking the sanction of sanitation, we even gave up for many years the most effective way of resuscitating the drowning, since it involved giving them our breath. We protect privacy with the sanction of health and sanitation; it is good to have a room of one's own and unhealthy to share it with five others. It used to be merely a question of enough fresh air; it has since been transformed into a question of mental health; whatever the sanction, it does ensure privacy.

In our society, clothing separates mother and child; is it to protect each from the hazards of a sudden draft? It was 102°F in my hospital room when I was first allowed to hold my baby; yet both baby and mother were carefully swathed in cloth which kept them to that degree distinct. Clothing, in fact, guards everyone against cutaneous contact with others, except perhaps, at the beach. We have divided our benches into individual units; our seats in school, on the train, on the bus. Even our solid sofas, planned for social groupings, have demarcating lines or separate pillows to help individuals keep apart. But the Tikopia help the self to be continuous with its society through their physical arrangements. They find it good to sleep side by side crowding each other, next to their children or their parents or their brothers and sisters, mixing sexes and generations; and if a widow finds herself alone in her one-room house, she may adopt a child or a brother to allay her intolerable privacy.

In our society, we protect ourselves from each other's secretions in the interest of sanitation. Who but very young children would think of sharing toothbrushes? But among the Tikopia, people like to chew the half masticated betel wads of others; and these are passed with affection from older to younger, from brother to sister.

In the area of food, also, we erect a sanitary barrier around the individual. A mother is urged never to taste food she cooks with the same spoon which she uses for stirring; and this, even though the temperature of the food is such that it oftentimes will kill any germs she might introduce from her mouth. Indeed, the disgust aroused if she acts otherwise may have less to do with the logic of sanitation, than with the thought that the mother's saliva might thus be introduced into the food. And, of course, when it comes to the care of infants, the mother is urged to be even more careful. So machinery chews the baby's food into a mash, bottlewarmers and other mechanical devices bring the child's food to body temperature, boiling water sterilizes away the mother's tactile contact, bottles and cups and spoons separate the mother from the mouth of the child.

The Tikopia mother phrases all feeding as physical continuity. If she is not suckling the child, she maintains this continuity in some other way. She masticates the solid food herself, partly digesting it with her saliva before bending down to put it into the baby's mouth with her lips, like a bird feeding its young. The water she gives the baby is also mixed with her saliva first and warmed with her own body warmth in her mouth, before it is given to the baby with her lips.

Something of this is carried on into the family meal—or rather household meal, for a number of other relatives often live in the house, or share the meal of the day. The older members are deliberately given portions too large for them, and the younger members portions too small, so that the elder can pass their leavings to the younger. It is not a question of neatly cutting off the portion one cannot eat, and putting it aside; the Tikopia use no tools other than their hands in eating. The leavings are passed on bearing the marks of the eaters' fingers, which, carefully licked clean, have slid down the side of the heap. And the guest from another district is given an enormous portion, so that he can have his own leavings to take home. This is not the same as taking a gift from the storehouse; this is taking a share of a social occasion away with him.

Work among the Tikopia is also socially conceived and structured; and if a man has to work alone, he will probably try to take a little child along. In our culture, the private office is a mark of status, an ideal; and a man has really arrived when he can even have a receptionist to guard him from any social intrusion without his private consent. Our kitchen planners, caught between ideals of privacy and efficiency on the one hand, and the new teachings of child specialists on the other, have not yet managed to introduce the child into the kitchen as anything much better than a necessary evil.

To the Tikopia, an American kitchen, with the mother mainly concerned with having everything within reach and no one under foot, would be an atrocity. When they prepare the meal, after they have returned from their gardening and other food-getting occupations, the whole Tikopia household works together. Nothing is within reach, and children fill this gap, fetching and carrying and running errands, forming a bridge between adult and adult. Father and mother, the unmarried aunt, the grandmother, the brother-in-law, all work together, firing the oven, scraping taro, grating coconut. One gets fiber for making a coconut strainer, another squeezes out the coconut cream, another is nursing the baby. While they wait for the food to bake, they carve cups out of coconut shell, or plait sinnet, or play. Jokes and anecdotes fly back and forth. No one apparently wants to be alone so as to concentrate or to work more efficiently.

The work situations which Raymond Firth presents always convey this joy and sheer satisfaction, at least to this reader. There seems to be no compulsion to work. When Firth speaks of "obligations," he probably does so to explain to his Western readers how it is that a man will work without external coercion of any sort. But we find the Tikopia often choosing these "obligations." For example, Firth tells how the husbands of women married out of a family group have the obligation to fire and tend the ovens when this family group performs a public celebration. He speaks too of the sons of widowed women, who are the guests of honor on such occasions, but who nevertheless choose to assume the role of their dead fathers and come instead as cooks; here is choice, not compulsion. People choose to make contributions to the donor during a great gift-giving occasion, even though they are to participate in the occasion as recipients, whether they have made a contribution or not. People manage to discover obscure avenues of relationship which will enable them to assume such "obligations"; this means that they will have to get and prepare and plait sinnet, or dig and scrape taro, or get pandannus and beat it into bark cloth; it also means a fuller participation and involvement in the social situation.

In our own culture, we do have what we call cooperative undertakings, and we urge parents to plan cooperative work for the family. But these are proposed ultimately for the benefit of the individual, so that the end is a collective end, not a common end. It would be a mistake to see the Tikopia situation as a cooperative one in this sense. Cooperation, like altruism, presupposes our own definition of a discrete self.

In the use they make of kinship terms, also, the Tikopia define the individual socially. Kinship terms, of course, always do define the individual on a social basis, and, to my knowledge, they are present in all societies. But not everywhere are they used as they are used among the Tikopia. Here the personal name is rarely used. Brothers and sisters call each other by kinship terms, and parents call their children "son" and "daughter" when they do not have to specify. In addressing or referring to older people, when specification is necessary, the name of the dwelling is used, such as "mother's brother from ———," not the personal name.

In the kind of terms which they choose to use, the Tikopia show the extent to which they view the individual as social. It seems to be a common practice, for example, to refer to, or address a relative, not in terms of his relation to oneself, but in terms of his relation to a common relative, thus widening the circle, and bringing in another relation by implication. A child, speaking to his mother's brother, will probably refer to his father as "your brother-in-law." A father may call out to his sons, "You brethren." A man may address his son-in-law as "You brother-in-law linked (that is, related as brother-in-law) to my son" thus evoking a fourth relative. A man may call his father-in-law *grandfather*-linked, thus introducing his own child into the term. And when non-kin speak of others who may be considered to be related to one another in however distant a manner, they often refer to them in terms of this mutual relationship, not in terms of who they are as individuals. For example, Firth tells of seeing two women going by, his asking who they were. The answer came: "They are father's-sister-linked" (they are a woman and her brother's daughter). Firth was asking for a definition of their identities; what he got was a completely social definition, and still did not know "who" they were. He adds that even when accepting the answer given he was left puzzled, because the relationship, when he finally worked it out, was so tenuous and obscure. Yet his informant chose this as the basis for his definition.

The individual is known also in terms of another definition. When he marries and is the head of a household, he and his wife are known by the name of their house plot. In fact, there is a continuity between *fenua* (land) and people which is evidenced in the use of the word. A man says, "My *fenua*, it is Tikopia," and he also says, "*Fenua* has made speech," and "*Fenua* is many" (many people are present). *Fenua* is also used to refer to the placenta.

This continuity with land-society has found expression, negatively and disastrously, in intense nostalgia during absence. Recruiting for plantation labor was prohibited in Tikopia when repeated experience showed that almost all the men died when away from home. On one occasion, the twenty men taken to Guadalcanal were absolved from all plantation work and allowed to fish all day by way of arousing in them an interest in life; but, in spite of this treatment, only one of the twenty survived to return to Tikopia. An attempt by the Melanesian Mission to send boys away to school in 1928 met with failure, and all three had to be sent back by the next boat.

The Tikopia are continuous with their dead society as well. Under the floor of their houses, or just outside beneath the eaves, dwell their dead relatives. The presence of the dead is taken for granted, and there is frequent communication with them. One long dead ancestor even became a Christian, as he happened to be inhabiting a living Tikopia at the time when this man was being baptized. A dead Tikopia who dwelt under the floor of Raymond Firth's house objected to the crowds who gathered when the ethnographer played the gramophone, and Firth had to give up this recreation. There may be merely a matter-of-fact awareness of the presence of the dead, or there may be specific contact in a dream, or through a medium.

The land "belongs" to the dead, and is under their care; so that their descendants walk carefully and in awareness on the land of their fathers. When a social offence is perpetrated, such as an incestuous marriage, it is the dead relatives who punish the living. At the beginning of a meal, some food is flung casually at the graves of the dead relatives; and, in fact, the relationship throughout has the casualness of an assured continuity. When the definite presence of a dead one is desired, a man will ask a medium to bring him for a visit. On one such occasion, Firth reports that the man who had issued the invitation had started on some occupation by the time his dead nephew arrived; so he simply asked the medium to offer the dead some betel nut and to tell him that his host was too busy to chew it with him.

The deities of the Tikopia are their early dead ancestors, so these also are eventually their relatives. They are addressed as grandparents, in terms implying a more relaxed relationship than the term for father or father's sister. They are treated with the same respect and concern accorded relatives. For example, Firth describes how an expert, repairing a canoe from which the three inhabiting deities had been removed lest they be disturbed by the disruption to their body, worked furiously against time and worried because the gods were being deprived of their body. It was a question of sympathy, not of currying favor. And with their gods, the Tikopia feel so comfortable that they play jokes on even the highest of them.

I have spoken of affection, sympathy, concern. The Tikopia have one word which covers these concepts and similar ones: *arofa*. Grief, gratitude, moral support, pride in, appreciation of another, all these are also included under this term. In fact, this is the term for social warmth, the social emotion, the continuity of which I have been speaking. *Arofa* and the acts of *arofa*, exist only among people who are socially continuous, kin and people who have shared living over a period of time. A man does not speak of feeling *arofa* for his sweetheart; in fact, the correct marriage is phrased as a violent and hostile abduction from the *arofa* group, separating an individual from it in the way a strand is removed from a cord. Later, however, there is *arofa* between husband and wife. A man dividing his property, his clubs and spears, sinnet belts and ornaments, among his sons and grandsons, feels that he will now be "properly present" in his descendants; and such heirlooms are *tau-arofa* (bond-of-arofa).[1] Men and women wear *tau-arofa* of dead and living relatives: teeth, bored and suspended on a cord; hair made into a circlet, a waistcloth. Women in particular wear circlets made of the hair of sons or brothers or husbands or fathers. These are visible forms of *arofa*.

Arofa exists in the concrete act, as the Tikopia say; and such acts are many. Whenever an individual is in a position of strain or crisis, *arofa* is shown by his relatives through physical contact. If a small child wanders away from his father and is frightened or hurt, he runs back to be held in his father's arms. When he is older, this same physical contact gives him comfort and support under similar circumstances. When a boy or girl appears for the first time at the sacred dances of Marae, male relatives on the mother's side crowd around the novice, shielding the dancer from the eyes of the curious, holding up his arms, going with him through the motions of the dance. When a Tikopia is ill, the mother's brother will come and offer his back as a support to the sick one, or hold him in his arms. A more inclusive group of relatives, representing the complete social unit, assembles thickly at a time of birth, marriage, death.

The continuity of the individual with the social unit is particularly in evidence during the rites of the Firing of the Ovens of Youth, when the operation of superincision is performed on the young boys who are being initiated into the society of men. Nowadays the operation is performed with a razor blade, but earlier a sharp shell was used; and, in any case, it is still a painful performance, particularly as the operator is often not expert and not sure. It is an introduction to the society of men, not an ordeal to try fortitude; and the whole procedure is imbued with *arofa* in so many specific ways, that, in the end, the boys are said not to feel pain at the time of the operation.

Preparation for the rites begins months before the occasion. From now on the coming rites color the life of the large group of kin. Gardens are planted because of the additional food needed, coconuts are used frugally with an eye to the coming rites. Sinnet is made into cords for gifts, mats are woven, bark cloth is beaten, the reef is dragged; the whole social unit is involved to a greater or lesser extent. A few days before the actual operation, the boy is invited to the houses of relatives. There he is given food and smeared with vermilion turmeric. At each household, a female relative

---

[1] I have found no term in English which will convey the meaning of *tau*. Firth, faced with this predicament, uses the word "linked," which, I think, implies even more strongly a prior separation. Consanguine and affinal kin as well as certain forms of "property" are referred to with *tau*.

gives him a new loincloth; and the boy removes the one he is wearing and gives it to her to tie around her neck, as an act of *arofa*. At this time, his relatives begin to practice the singing of dirges whose general theme is *arofa*. In the meantime, taro is being dug by groups of men, women, and children, food is being collected in a huge pile, and preparations are being completed.

On the day of the operation, the boy continues the visiting of relatives, who smear him with turmeric and give him new waistcloths as before. From early morning the assembled relatives sing dirges, mourning the shedding of the boy's blood, the injury to his flesh. As one group finishes, another group takes up the mourning. Men wail and sob, beating their breasts, women cut themselves with knives and gouge their flesh with their nails. By this time, the relatives have laid the boy's pain on their own necks, they have injured their own flesh, they have wept and mourned for his pain and injury. Those who were not mourning have been busy working for the great gift-giving which is the main part of these rites. They have been plaiting sinnet, grating taro, peeling bananas, kneading, working together.

It is finally time for the operation, the occasion for all the preparations. The boy is carried into the house on the back of his mother's brother, dressed in a new waistcloth by female relatives, and covered with beads and other valuables. His uncle carries him to the place of operation, and sits holding him in his arms. Around them presses the group of near relatives, body close against body, giving support in this period of crisis. A general wailing began when the boy was brought to the house, and now the women are crying gently. Everyone has wailed and mourned, except the boy. His pain, his fear, his injury have been shared by all, diffused in time and in space through the *arofa* of his group.

There is no song of rejoicing when the operation is over; there is no singling out of the boy. If there is any feeling of achievement, it is that of the leader of the rites, who says, "Our work is good, let us sit and chew betel." The group plunges into an intricate series of gift-giving situations, which, according to Firth, are the most important event of the day. The boy, on this important day when he receives this painful mark of his initiation into the status of manhood, has furnished merely the occasion for a particularly intense and prolonged social participation. Now comes an extensive web of contributions to the main gift which has been prepared by many people over a period of months. There are gifts and countergifts, according to established structure, until everyone has had an active share in the great gift-giving occasion. As the mats and barkcloths will be distributed to every household, carrying with them some contact are received, the boy is made to lie between them; subsequently, these with the boy. In this and other ways, the boy comes eventually in touch with his whole social unit.

Such are the occasions marking the new status which comes from an introduction into the widening circle of adult society; in their function, they may be compared to commencement in our society, or to the Bar Mitzvah. Yet no individual achievement is celebrated; though many gifts are given and received, none are given to the boy himself and for himself, except for the transient flow of loincloths. Thus, while the boy is the occasion for the rites, the main focus is the involvement of the whole society in the ceremony.

Before the incision rites, another occasion has been celebrated in a mild way in the growing boy's life; this was his first experience of torch-light fishing. At this time, also, no one is concerned with the boy's achievement, and in fact he has achieved nothing except that he has joined a crew. He is not even given a torch to hold or a net to use. He merely paddles with the rest of the crew; and it is this step in increasing socialization which is marked with a firing of the ovens, and a gift-giving. Social development, not increased individuation, is celebrated and the only gift given to the boy is one which he is to take to his parents.

Society appears as the referent in other ways. The commonest curse, used casually and without offence, is a "social" one: "May your father eat filth." Even fathers use this to their children. Birth control and infanticide are carried on in the name of society, so that there should be enough for all. Gift exchanges are carried on in such a way that everyone in the unit participates in giving; gifts from a household are announced in the names of all, including those of the young children. If some giver's name is omitted by some oversight, some relative may whisper to have one of his gifts announced in the name of the slighted giver, so that this man, too, can have a share in the occasion.

With such a definition of the self within the medium of *arofa*, work can take place among the Tikopia without coercion, without the incentive of reward or the fear of punishment, without the spur of individual profit; because work as participation is meaningful.

REFERENCES

Firth, Raymond. *We, The Tikopia*. New York: American Book Company, 1936.

————. *The Work of the Gods in Tikopia*. London: Lund, Humphries & Co., Ltd., 1940.

————. *Primitive Polynesian Economy*. New York: Humanities Press, 1950.

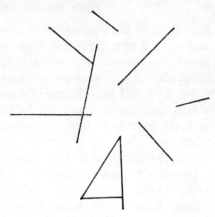

Equality of Opportunity
as a Cultural Value

EQUALITY OF OPPORTUNITY IS A COM-
mon phenomenon, present in many societies throughout the world. What
is rare is to find equality upheld consciously as a tenet, as it is in the Western world, as a principle to be deliberately applied. My thesis here is
that the principle of equality is adequate to democracy only when it derives naturally from the tenet of the dignity of man, only when it is a by-
product of the absolute and permeating respect for human worth. In the
Western world, at any rate in recent years, the roles of these two principles
have been reversed to a certain extent; equality has not been viewed as
incidental to respect for individual worth, but has been considered instead as a measure to bring about respect for human worth. To this extent,
it has been for the West not an inalienable aspect of the respect for man,
not necessary to the definition of democracy, but rather something addi-
tive and external—something to be applied, or a means to achieve a desired end.

If it is to be a true democratic principle, equality must derive from pos-
tulates such as those formulated by Albert Hofstadter, particularly, "Every

From *Aspects of Human Equality*, Fifteenth Symposium of the Conference on Science,
Philosophy and Religion, New York, 1956.

human being has intrinsic dignity, infinite worth, incomparable and ultimate." As it operates in the American scene, to my mind, equality often rests on the opposite assumption: that man is finite and comparable. This assumption may give rise to discriminatory inequality as well, and to self-seeking and other-belittling competitiveness. Upon this assumption, a man is measurable and can be evaluated on the basis of comparison with others; that is, he is not infinite, and is not valued as of ultimate worth.

Equality in this sense is perhaps useful as an intermediate measure, as a necessary step in the abolition of the ills of inequality; it can be used to ensure that in the end men will have the opportunity to function with dignity. But it is not enough, because it cannot go beyond this. Based as it is on comparable measurement of the finite, it has a feedback which enhances the concept of the measurability of man. In this era of groupism, there is eventual danger in this feedback—danger that the uniqueness of the individual will be lost sight of, giving place to the tenet of interchangeability, one of the cornerstones of totalitarianism. What we need is a feedback which will generate and enhance respect for human dignity, which will naturally bring about full equality; otherwise, equality will need a huge machinery to maintain it, perhaps even legal coercion, thus bringing about the violation of human dignity.

I have arrived at this position through the study of other societies where equality exists in the very nature of things, as a by-product of the democratic structure of the culture itself, not as a principle to be applied. In such societies, there is no attempt to achieve the goal of equality, and in fact, there is no concept of equality. Often, there is no linguistic mechanism whatever for comparison. What we find is absolute respect for man, for all individuals irrespective of age and sex.

In this country, equality has been interpreted variously. It has meant sometimes that rights were to be apportioned meticulously in accordance with what an individual already had, say, in terms of property or position. This was the basic principle according to which common lands were apportioned in the towns of seventeenth-century New England: one acre to him who had one, ten to him who had ten. In this instance, equality meant strict adherence to a common basis of measure; equality of proportion, rather than equality of object. Another interpretation of equality stresses sameness of rights, as when every child throughout the state or the country is compelled to avail himself of the same number of years of formal schooling, irrespective of what he is or has or wants or is able to take. This is a concern with fairness in disregard of individual peculiarity, as when we give the same number of lemon drops to each child, hungry or satiated, happy or in need of comforting, plump or lean, greedy or generous or a hoarder. In the name of equality women in this country have sought sameness of role, demanding the same rights, privileges, opportunities as men. In its name we may seek equivalence, as between performance and reward, crime and punishment.

We may find equality incorporated in an average, expressed in conformity, and thus all individual difference, all "inequality" considered as deviation. The varying conceptions of equality have this in common: all are based on comparison and measurement of some kind. All begin, not with the individual case, not with the person in his "dignity," but with an overall principle, a standard externally set and applied; a standard chosen because it can be commonly applied without deviation, because it is fair and symmetrically just. It is this meaning in which I use the term equality when I discuss equality of opportunity below, and the concept of equality itself. I should like to raise the question here as to whether the principle of equality, used to evaluate and assign in terms of measure and comparison, is in fact adequate in affording opportunity in a truly democratic way. If freedom is necessary to the definition of democracy, then I would maintain that the principle of equality—in the sense in which I use the term—is opposed to the democratic ideal. Its essence is at variance with freedom, which can be realized only when human dignity is valued without measure, and when the rights of others are respected in their integrity, without comparison or a utilitarian calculus.

This view of equality is challenged as a democratic principle by many non-Western cultures, in which a democratic way of life is actualized without reference to the notion of equality. The societies where we find these cultures, afford opportunity to their members, as well as the freedom to avail themselves of the opportunity; however, they do this in ways which run counter to our own equalitarian principles.

Throughout the world we find societies as in the Pacific, among the Bantu in Africa and Indians in North America, where human dignity is maintained inviolate, freedom of the individual is facilitated, and full opportunity—within the limits of the cultural resources—is afforded to the members of the society, in the absence of any concern for equality. This does not mean that we find therefore the absence of inequality, but that whatever inequality—in our own view—may be present is irrelevant to evaluation, being viewed merely as another kind of difference, to be recognized and accepted as valid. What we call unfairness in an individual may be accepted as legitimate partiality, as the idiosyncrasy of the individual. Equality here is not needed to ensure the dignity of man, because man is valued in completely different terms. In fact, even the notion itself of equality is not universally present throughout the societies of the world; and concepts which make it possible for us to think in terms of differential levels and averages, of equality and inequality, are often also absent in their cultural framework

In the Western world, we have in our system of thought, notions and attitudes which predispose us to evaluation in terms of equality. Assessment and even apprehension of objects of knowledge in terms of comparison, is fundamental to our thinking. We know that a thing is *good* because we recognize it *as good as* or *better than*; we know that an infant is tall or slow only when we know his age, that is, when we can compare him with the infants in his age-group. We define accordng to similarities and dissimilarities, according to qualities which can be analyzed and abstracted out of the field under consideration. For example, John Plamenatz writes: "Everyone knows that, whatever the respect in which we choose to compare men, some will be superior to others." This may be true when we do choose certain respects in which to compare men. But there are societies where no one is "superior to others," not because the goal of equality has been successfully achieved, not because all men are born with equal ability, but because two fundamental premises necessary to this proposition are lacking: the notion of comparison is not present, and neither is the practice of choosing a "respect" out of the totality of the individual.

To compare at all, we have to choose a "respect," because comparison is possible only after analysis and abstraction. I can compare an apple to a pear, and find it equal or superior or inferior in regard to smoothness of skin, sweetness, texture, juiciness, color; but apprehended in their totality, the two are unique and noncomparable. And we do find a number of cultures where being is apprehended and understood in this way; that is, in its integrity, without reference to what it is like or unlike, without analysis into constituents. Such is the culture of the Trobrianders of the South Pacific, in whose language we find almost a total absence of adjectives, since the goodness of a yam is different from the goodness of a gardener or a canoe, being an inextricable ingredient of the unique whole. This language offers no mechanism for comparison; it offers instead a large number of terms for what would be for us the same object with varying qualities or even varying degrees of the same quality. For instance, the yam of appropriate ripeness for harvesting is termed a *taytu*, but for the not-quite-ripe and the over-ripe there are completely different terms. The difference is not one of degree; it is an aspect of uniqueness. People desire to be *good* (or rather good-gardeners); not *better than*. A gardener works much and hard because he was strong, because he enjoyed gardening, because he wanted to participate largely in the gift-giving situations. Neither he nor others made a practice of evaluating his work against a comparative standard of achievement or expectation. Striving was not for equality nor for superiority; it was for the enhancement of uniqueness. A man boasted: "I stand alone; I am the only one." What might be seen as "competition" was rather a public demonstration of performance, an exhibit where everyone did his utmost in concert. So at the canoe launching ceremonial, the canoes—old and new and newly repaired—all went out in the water while the crowd of spectators on the beach enjoyed the spectacle. They did not travel an equal distance, nor an equal length of time; and the time of return was not recorded; if they were compared at all, the comparison was not evaluative. It was apparently possible for the Trobrianders to compare; at any rate they did seek to achieve equivalence upon occasion. But they did this only in situations which were absolutely without value, as when they bartered, an activity which they despised. Measurement was also present; but it was used only as a convenience, not on principle; and the notion of the average as a standard of measure did not exist.

Throughout the history of the Western world, inequality has given rise to the relationship of subordination-superordination, inferiority-superiority. It has made it possible for master to order servant, for ruler to coerce subject. We have upheld the principle of equality by way of correcting these evils. Yet elsewhere these evils have been absent even though the notion of equality was also absent. In the Burmese village of the past century, the great value set on personal autonomy and the respect for the autonomy of each and everyone, insured the absence of these relationships. Here a farmer reportedly could not hire labor, as no one could be subservient to another man.

In this continent, the Wintu Indians of California embodied in their culture a conception of democracy beyond that which our own ideal encompasses. Here man was conceived as coordinate with man and nature; there was no hierarchy conferring differential respect and privilege. The chief exhorted the people, but never commanded, except when he was requested to as an emergency measure when an enemy attacked. The Wintu phrase which my informant felt obliged to translate into English as: the chief *ruled* the people, is given in Wintu as: the chief *stood-with* the people. The relationship of coordination, the democracy of the culture, is implemented throughout the grammar of the language. The verbal suffixes which we would automatically see as transitivizers, express instead the relationship of coordination or sharing or cooperation; to do *to*, is rendered in Wintu as: to do *with*, or to share an experience with. So, what is for us "I watched him," is for the Wintu, "I watched with him." Possession, having, is for the Wintu: "to live with." What I translated as: "I want to cure my son," was stated as: "I want to participate in my son's recovery." "I fed my child," is for the Wintu: "I participated in my child's eating." These coordinative and participative suffixes are employed in relation to animals and plants also; only rarely are terms expressive of the imposition of the self on the other to be found in the texts which I recorded. The Wintu believe that a man kills game only with the consent of the deer or bear or salmon; and so, a man may say either: "I could not kill any deer," or "Deer don't want to die for me." To my mind this is the essence of democracy; yet here, also, it does not rest on the principle of equality. The Wintu are people who, like the Trobrianders, do not compare individuals with one another, or against a standard. In all the mythological and ethnographic material which I recorded, and in the texts which give brief descriptions of individuals, I find no spontaneous comparison made, either in describing or in assessing; nor are individuals described in comparative terms in the brief character sketches I recorded. The language affords a mechanism for comparison, but this, I think, is used only once in my texts, when some children are urged to go *further* north. And I have recorded no terms referring to equality.

Here and among the Trobrianders, equality itself is present, I think; that is, we find the fact of equality, as a dimension in relationships, as an aspect of the opportunity to be, to function. But its existence is derivative; it is not a goal, but is incidental to some other basic concept. It derives from the recognition of the right to be different, noncommensurate, unique; from the valuing of sheer being. When it is being itself which is valued, then none can be inferior or superior; would it be nonsense to say this is because all being equally *is*? If absolute fullness of opportunity is afforded, if the culture facilitates and implements freedom, thus making it possible for the individual to avail himself of his opportunity, then equality of opportunity may be said to be present, since all have fullness of opportunity. But here equality of opportunity does not rest on measure or comparison or the principle of fairness.

In fact, in our own culture, when we seek to establish equality of rights in the name of democracy, we often mean this fullness I have spoken of, not a measured equality of opportunity. I believe that this is what John

Plamenatz has in mind when he writes "To believe in equality is to believe that there are some rights common to all men so much more important than other rights that these others ought always, or nearly always, to be sacrificed to them, should the need arise. It is to believe that no social institutions and no privileges are morally defensible if they make it impossible or especially difficult for any part of the community to exercise those rights." This is no preoccupation with measured equality, but with fullness without measure, with significance—can significance be equalized or compared?—with concern with the integrity of man's rights, not with their extent.

To my mind, the application of the principle of equality in the form of an externally set standard of measure, has sometimes led to deprivation from the very opportunity which we seek to afford equally. It has led to inequality in the "significant" right of each to develop inner potentiality and uniqueness. In such cases, equality does not result in opportunity, but in coercion. When I force all children of ten, in a certain city, to study fractions in April, I am doing so in the name of equality of opportunity; but what exactly do I achieve? There are the children who, unready, incapable, uninterested, are constrained by this "opportunity." There are the children who, bored with the easy work are nevertheless—in the name of democracy—forbidden to move beyond, since this would introduce inequality, or point to the ignored inequality of native endowment. Some of our thinkers are now rightly concerned with the paradox of "compulsory free" education, according to which we coerce our children to go through the motions of availing themselves of the equality of opportunity to be educated.

The recognition and acceptance of difference as valid and as neither degrading nor elevating, would avoid this dilemma. Such recognition of uniqueness is not the same, I think, as the goal of "personality fulfilled" which John Plamenatz decries as smacking of the doctrine of final causes. However, it also differs from the alternative he suggests: "Every society imposes some kind of discipline on its members, and this discipline, acting upon their natural dispositions, makes them the persons they are." I do not think that all societies "impose." Some offer culture, not as a binding standard, but as a guide for procedure. For these, discipline increases opportunity; and there is no equalitarian standard of expectation from the members of the society. One can say that every society offers to its members a framework for experience and action—a map of beaten paths through the jungle of living. Some societies use coercive measures to move the individual along these paths of culture. They have rigid expectations of performance; they evaluate the progress of one man against that of another. They reward according to distance covered. Others are concerned only in seeing that each individual is enabled to set out on his own chosen path, among those offered by the culture; and when he errs into the jungle, or when he stumbles, the society does not judge nor punish, but may even help the individual to use this misstep toward a richer progress. Such is the society of the Lovedu about which I shall speak below. There is limitation of opportunity here only in the sense that the paths are limited; here man is free to stray, but if he goes beyond the point where the society can help him, he is lost.

Everywhere, in every society, the culture offers its peculiar codification of reality, its peculiar avenues of experience. Some societies may "impose," "act upon," "make" their members the persons they are. Others do not *make*, but help their members *to be*; they enable them to select, within the limits of the structure, the raw material they need for their own unique growth. In such societies, individuals set their conduct according to an internal standard, not according to external expectancies. I believe this is what is meant in the *Bhagavad Gita*: "The law of one's own nature, though devoid of merit is preferable to the Dharma of another though well performed." "Death in one's own law of nature is better for man than victory in an alien movement. To follow the law of another nature is dangerous to the soul, contradictory as we may say to the natural way of his evolution, a thing mechanically imposed and therefore imported, artificial and sterilizing to one's own growth towards the true nature of the spirit." The concept of equality is irrelevant to this view of man. Here we have instead the full valuing of man in his uniqueness, enabling him to actualize himself, to use opportunity fully, undeterred by the standards of an outside authority, not forced to deviate, to meet the expectations of others.

The principle of equality, in the sense in which I have been discussing it, arises from the same premises that also give rise to symmetrical relations, and to competition as fundamental to incentive, goal, and standard of performance. These premises are not confined to the Western world. We find comparability according to measured value among the Bella Coola of British Columbia, for example. In this society, to give a gift meant to enhance the giver's value to a clearly measured degree, and to belittle the value of the receiver to exactly that degree. To grow in value, the receiver had to give back a much larger gift, receiving an even larger one eventually; so that inequality was maintained through the very structure of the society. Hamed Ammar, writing of his native village in Upper Egypt, speaks of comparison and rivalry there as accepted methods in child-rearing; so that even a visitor will greet a child with the question: Who is better, you or your brother?

We have further those societies where, as Lyman Bryson puts it, inequality is institutionalized; that is, where the difference in status and privilege inheres in the very structure. Yet often, in these cases, there is inequality only from the viewpoint of a comparative standard. Otherwise, what we see as inequality, may be instead a difference in kind, not in degree. It may be the immutable difference of caste, or of rank, or of sex status; it may be the privilege differential which changes with age status, or other progressive social status, as where a daughter-in-law is subservient to her husband's mother, but eventually becomes a mother-in-law herself, maintaining the difference in status but changing her position in the structure. The difference may be accepted and even valued as a given, or it may be a potential or a festering source of friction; from a humanistic point of view, it may be grossly unjust. However it may be regarded, this type of difference always means that the fullness of opportunity is not society-wide, but exists only within a specified status, limited by the definition of this status. Yet in all these cases, it is hazardous to assess on the basis of a comparative measure; after all, the Untouchables in India were privileged to have in certain respects a much freer life and certainly a more interesting diet—from our point of view—than the Brahmins with their many restrictions.

In this country, the Hopi Indians of Arizona traditionally extended this principle of differentiation to the entire universe. Difference in status was found in society and in the cosmic whole; yet equality here was implicit in the structure of the universe itself. All aspects of the universe were "equally" significant, as they were all indispensable: clouds, pollen, eagles, rattlesnakes, salt, turquoise, each recognized color and cardinal direction, each man and woman, child and adult. Each had his own role, his unique function; each was "incomparable and ultimate." Ideally, each aspect of the universe helped maintain the cosmic order; and in accordance with this principle, individuals helped one another within the family and the pueblo, trying to relate themselves in a spirit of harmony and cooperation. Men prepared and performed ceremonials, to help the sun move along his established path or to help the corn move through the pattern of its growth.

The ideal of mutual helpfulness, of full opportunity, of harmony, was associated with a dislike of outstandingness, as of something which caused the individual to become separate from the supporting group. This, in turn, may be viewed in our terms as equality; but equality itself was not a goal. It became a goal negatively, when it was threatened by the competition which the Whites attempted to introduce, as, for example, through the school system. Then the child who was more quick, more able or careful than the rest, devised ways in which he could avoid being outstanding, not because inequality was morally wrong, but because it was emotionally discomforting. The equality present among the Hopi was not based on comparison; it was not an achieved equality, it was not aimed at removing evils of inequality. Competitive success was not sought, in fact was not good, so there was no achieved inequality. Opportunity was neither measured nor equalized, but was afforded in full to be utilized according to individual capacity within the structured role.

In the Western world, the principle of equality has been necessary to ensure that all shall have opportunity. If all are to have freedom of opportunity, the freedom of each must be limited so that there should be no interference, no encroachment upon the freedom of others; and equality was evoked as the principle upon which the limits to the freedom of each should be decided. In a society in which individual is pitted against individual, either in competition or in the interest of conformity, and where justice lies in apportionment according to similar measure, it was natural that freedom of opportunity should be translated into equality of opportunity. Equality was the solution appropriate to a culture where self is opposed to other, where society has to be protected from the encroachment of the individual; the solution of a society which holds an either-or conception of duality. There are societies, however, where dualism is complementary, so that the terms of the duality are not opposed nor measured against each other, nor seem as discrete units. I give a brief sketch below of such a society where the principle of equality was not necessary to freedom of opportunity: the society of the Lovedu of South Africa which E. and J. Krige studied in the thirties.

In this society, equality as principle was not needed, and it could exist as a concept because the self was not opposed to the other, nor assessed against the other, nor compared to the other. The self was related to the other in conciliation, and formed with the other a whole in process, maintained through continuing reciprocities. The freedom of an individual did not have to be protected against interference from another individual who was exercising his freedom; it had been safeguarded by the tremendous respect accorded to individual worth, and by the great value for relationships of mutuality, so that even an act of overt aggression would be transformed in this society into the first act of a relationship of reciprocity.

Here the individual was viewed as unique, noncomparable, non measurable. This meant, on the one hand, that there were no standards of expectation to meet, no average against which an individual was assessed, no competitive standard of success. On the other hand, it meant that equality did not have a place; in fact, it was bad to seek equivalence, which smacked of measurement and calculation, the attributes of the abominated commercialism of the Europeans. It meant that compensation, reward, payment, punishment, as we know them, were absent in this culture.

A corollary to the respect for individual uniqueness and worth was that the individual was held to be inviolate. The freedom of the individual was thus again guarded from encroachment. The exercise of force of any kind, except in dealing with the very young infant, was never approved. Even a court of law refrained from executing its decision, on the principle that to do so would be to coerce and was therefore to be avoided. The parties involved were expected to work out matters between them, aiming at a conciliatory solution, implementing the court decision through mutual agreement. The culprit, if there was one, was left to pay restitution at his own pace. He might merely make evident his willingness to do so, or might perhaps pay only a part and promise to "look for" the rest. The willingness and the promise were enough to rehabilitate the offender. Preferably, however, matters were not allowed to come to the point where they had to be submitted to a court decision. The court preferred merely to arbitrate and clarify, not to condemn or suggest restitution. If an individual wronged another either deliberately or accidentally, it was the usual practice for him to send a conciliator to express regret and to offer a goat of pardon. And when matters were brought to court, this procedure was urged first of all, as the preferred solution. Condemnation was avoided as violating the individual, and as not leading to rehabilitation; and punishment was bad as it meant retribution involving equivalence. The complainant who insisted on the pinning of guilt and on restitution, was condemned, therefore, as vengeful; that is, as seeking equivalence.

In all matters, the Lovedu held that the event succeeding the offense, that is the consequence of the crime, should be, not punishment, but conciliation. If a man committed homicide for instance, the preferred way of dealing with this situation was for the culprit to offer his sister to the victim as wife. This initiated a life-long relationship, in fact a relationship extending endlessly in time, in which the family of the culprit and of his male descendants would be giving brides to the family of the victim, and receiving cattle from them. The relationship would be expressed in a series of reciprocities: visits would be periodically exchanged between the two households, the women of the bride's family bringing large amounts of beer and receiving goats from the family of the bridegroom, as well as other gifts and services. This is the consequence of a murder; it carries us a long way from the principle of an eye for an eye.

The Kriges describe a case where a young woman was "punished": a young mother performs an act allowed only within the role of a grandmother. The grandmother, outraged, consults her age-group—that is, the grandmothers of her village and neighboring villages—and they decide to punish the young mother and her age-group. The first step is for the young group to make and bring beer for all to drink—the medium of reconciliation, and mutuality; the symbol of sociability. As a second step, a beating is administered; the oldest grandmother beats the next oldest grandmother, and so on down the line to the youngest mother; after this, the grandmothers deliver a lecture, and the occasion is over. The offense has been used as an opportunity for conciliation, sharing, sociability.

In all areas of living, equivalence—depending as it does on measurement and comparison—was lacking. In the so-called exchange of brides for cattle, there was no idea of calculating the worth of one in terms of the other. The number of cattle given had been established by the previous marriages of past generations—by the number of cattle which were given for the mother of the bride, and for her grandmother, and great-grandmother in this particular line; the number did not change with the attractiveness or youth or desirability of the bride. Throughout the ages, these two families have continued and will continue to give—one brides, the other cattle; and will continue a relationship of countless reciprocities. These were valued in themselves, irrespective of extent or degree. To assess the service or the gift given as against that received, was abhorrent.

How can there be fairness in business dealings under these circumstances? The answer is that there were no such dealings; the despised "bismis" relations were left to the Christians. A Lovedu man never hired out as a farm hand except in extremity; and he found the work particularly hard, because he now had to apply an external measure to it; he had to work in the field as long as his master did. The usual practice, when help was needed, was to invite people to an agricultural beer-party, a *lejema*. A large amount of beer was prepared over a period of days by the women of the household, and distributed in a great convivial gathering when work in the fields was over for the day. The people invited might stay away without apology, or might promise to come and not turn up; because a promise was not binding or compelling, but rather was accepted as an expression of willingness. In fact, there was nothing binding about the *lejema*. People came as they liked, when they liked, and worked each at his own rhythm. In the end, whether a man had worked hard the whole day, or had strolled in at the eleventh hour, he shared "equally" in the beer party.

Here, again, any equivalence of reward to achievement is irrelevant; in fact, if it appeared, it would be grossly destructive, degrading a social relationship into commercialism. For the Lovedu, achievement must never be assessed, and people were not valued in terms of achievement. People were valued for what they were, for their personal qualities, such as maturity, experience, sagacity—not for the results of these qualities. It was not technical skill or perfection of performance which was admired, but rather the quality of industriousness, and the willingness to use one's possibly mediocre skill in helping. What was good was to promise, not necessarily to fulfill; to show willingness to pay one's debts rather than to pay them; so long as people were "looking for" the cattle or the goats they owed, they were not delinquent, even though they never found these.

Opportunity for self-fulfillment, according to the desire of each individual, was afforded to young and old. There was no expectation of achievement to be met. Children grew at their own pace, and were allowed to differ as they pleased; they were not assessed against an average. Parents took the children's contribution seriously, according it respect. not tolerance or indulgence. The calabash of the little girl of five might be small, but the water could be added profitably to the water the mother brought; and "the stick even of a child helps the adult across." The ownership rights of a child were respected, and if he had made a garden, he could dispose of the produce as he pleased. Children could go about as they pleased, though some pressure might be brought upon them on the part of their age group. If a child went off and did not return for the night, the parents assumed that he was visiting relatives in another village. The freedom to follow one's own bent was not endangered by comparison of one child to another as to attainments, physical size or abilities. There was neither suggestion nor encouragement of rivalry, which, among the Lovedu, seemed to be recognized only among co-wives. People found their self-expression in expanding responsibility, not in worsting a rival. They could not understand the rivalry among European children, their aggressiveness and inability to play together amicably.

It is meaningless to speak of the principle of equality in this picture. There is certainly fullness of opportunity for all, but if equality is present it is derivative. Inequality is either irrelevant, or is accepted difference

Reciprocity is only incidentally symmetrical. Freedom from interference is ensured through the absolute respect for the rights of others, through the high value of cooperation and mutuality, and through the genius for using uniqueness and difference to generate vital, self-sustaining relationships. In everyday life, in the law court, in the pervading system of marital "exchanges" there is conciliation without levelling, agreement without conformity, reciprocity without precisely calculated equivalences. Cooperation and harmony pervade the very structure of the culture, so that self-expression and self-fulfillment can find their fullest scope within the cooperative situation, in terms of helpfulness, of sharing, of respect for the inviolability of the rights of the others.

REFERENCES

Ammar, Hamed. *Growing Up in an Egyptian Village: Silwa, Province of Aswan.* London: Routledge & Kegan Paul, Ltd., 1954.

Krige, E. Jensen and J. D. Krige. *The Realm of a Rain-Queen. A Study of the Pattern of Lovedu Society.* New York: Oxford University Press, 1943.

McIlwraith, T. F. *The Bella Coola Indians.* Toronto: University of Toronto Press, 1948.

Mead, Margaret and Martha A. Wolfenstein (ed.). *Childhood in Contemporary Cultures.* Chicago: University of Chicago Press, 1955.

Thompson, Laura. *Culture in Crisis. A Study of the Hopi Indians.* New York: Harper & Brothers, 1950.

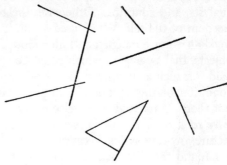

What Kind of Freedom?

IN THIS ESSAY I SPEAK OF THE IDEA of freedom which is peculiar to American society; I am not concerned with the ultimate question of what freedom is. As a concept or as a recognized value, freedom is rarely if ever present in non-Western cultures; but the thing itself, freedom, is certainly often present and carefully implemented—as autonomy, or otherwise as a dimension of the self. In this country, on the other hand, we do have the notion of freedom, and an ideal image of ourselves as "free." Ours is the "land of the free," we are born "free and equal"; and certainly, when these phrases were originally used, *free* referred to something of value beyond price, worth fighting and dying for.

A few years ago, with this in mind, I proceeded to find out how we use the term *free* in the mid-twentieth century. I had been struck by the increasing use of the term "I have to" or "I gotta," and wanted to find out in what areas Americans still expressed a sense of freedom in their linguistic usage. After weeks of listening to conversations of college and high school students, and of reading novels, articles and plays, I came

From *The Humanist*, American Humanist Association, Yellow Springs, Ohio, No. 4, 1958.

reluctantly to the conclusion that the term *free* was almost never used, except by people whose function it was to evoke or facilitate freedom, or to remind people about freedom, or to prod people into being concerned about it—that is, by people such as social scientists, politicians, psychoanalysts, and educators. Otherwise, the term *free* was not applied to the freedom of the self. When used at all, it was used occasionally to refer to freedom from entanglement, and more frequently, to free time and free objects, that is, objects which could be acquired or enjoyed without being paid for, such as free lectures or free cigars. *Free* here referred merely to a condition of the situation, a negative condition; to something that was not there. It referred to a welcome lack of requirement, to an absence of *have to*. I *do not have to* pay for the cigars, or for a ticket to attend the lecture; my time is free because I *do not have to* do anything now.

I found that the lack of requirement was welcome; yet it did not hold value. When I considered the attitude toward free objects, I discovered that to get a free ride, or to collect a large number of free samples, was perceived as a "break," or was a sign of one's ingenuity, but it did not enhance one's value; and a free cigar, however welcome and however good, held less value than the one for which a man *had to* pay a dollar. The violinist who charged and could get a high fee for his concert had more value than the one who offered to play "for free."

When it came to free time, it seemed, on the face of it, that this was certainly valued. People are constantly trying to achieve it. The increasing use of automatic machines in the home, for example, is more than labor-saving; it also achieves time-saving. It provides more free time for the housewife. Yet it seems to me that free time is valued only as *freed* time—time freed from the schedules and requirements to which the rest of one's time is committed. I find that when people say, "I am free," they usually mean, "I have some uncommitted time." This is a statement of fact, neither good nor bad; but to say that one is free all the time is not acceptable as a mere statement. One has to go on and give an explanation or a justification for such freedom, so as to endow it with a validity which is certainly not self-evident. The person who has nothing that he *has to do*, the person who can do what he presumably merely wants to do all the time, seems to be suspect, or to be pitied; or he is someone to worry about. He is not automatically valued for having all his time free. Is he a playboy, or unemployed, or incompetent, or ill, or over age? Conversely, I hear people speaking proudly of all they *have to do*, whether they are referring to committed time, or to what they do during their "free time."

In addition, as in the case of free objects, the *free* in free time appears to refer to a negative condition. In this case, free refers to emptiness; so that free time comes to be time to be filled. Our free time is "leisure" time, potentially passive and empty—and subject to boredom, unless we plan it carefully and fill it with activities. In fact, we have now a number of professions whose function it is to provide means and aid to people for the filling of empty time. And our increasing leisure is viewed with apprehension by many of our leaders. Our gerontologists have long been concerned over the increasing span of the age of leisure. More recently, our labor leaders have been worrying over the amount of leisure time which automation is bound to afford to the industrial workers. David Riesman, who was consulted about this looming problem, sees it not only as a case of having to fill empty time, but, more seriously, as a question of how to endow free-time activities with the value which is present in the non-free, "have-to" activities. As he sees it, even freed time—the free time of people whose time is otherwise regularly committed now, or has been committed in earlier years—is not highly valued. The freedom to choose does not contain value with which to endow the leisure-time activities which have been contrived to fill the free time.

Basic to all this is a conception of time and space which, if not peculiar to American culture, is certainly not common in non-Western thought. In Western thought—and I speak here of the view of the unsophisticated —space is empty and to be occupied with matter; time is empty and to be filled with activity. In both primitive and civilized non-Western cultures, on the other hand, free space and time have being and integrity. It was this conception of *nothingness* as *somethingness* that enabled the philosophers of India to perceive the integrity of non-being, to name the free space and give us the zero. In such societies, children are raised to listen to silence as well as sound. Luther Standing Bear, describing his childhood as an Oglalla Dakota in the eighteen-seventies, wrote: "[Children] . . . were taught to sit still and enjoy it. They were taught to use their organs of smell, to look when apparently there was nothing to see, and to listen intently when all seemingly was quiet. . . ." And Modupe, writing of his So-So childhood in French Guinea, says, "We learned that silences as well as sounds are significant in the forest and how to listen to the silences. . . . Deeply felt silences might be said to be the core of our Kofon religion. During these times, the nature within ourselves found unity with the nature of earth." In 1948, Virginia Lewisohn Kahn reported on the comfortable and not-empty silences of the Navaho women she visited—silences which at first disquieted her. The Wintu Indians have a suffix to refer to alert non-activity, to a silent, non-mobile commitment to awareness; a suffix I have found impossible to translate because there is no equivalent concept in American culture.

In Japanese traditional culture, free time and space are perceived as the *ma,* the valid interval or meaningful pause. Such perception is basic to all experience, and specifically to what constitutes creativity and freedom in the framework of Japanese culture. This perception apparently persists, in spite of the adoption of Western culture and science. Even in 1958, Misako Miyamoto wrote of the Noh-plays: "The audience watches the play and catches the feeling through not only the action and words but also the intervals of the period of pauses. . . . There is a free creation in each person's mind . . . ; and the audience relates to this situation with free thinking." Of silent intervals in speech, she says, "Especially [in] the pauses in a tone of voice, I can feel the person's unique personality and his joy, sorrow or other complicated feelings." On listening to a robin in early spring: "It sang with pauses. . . . I could have time to think about the bird [in] the silent moment between one voice and others. . . . The pauses produced the effect of the relation between the bird and me." In *The Integrity of the Interval,* Emilio Lanier—reversing this process—tried in 1956 to explain to Japanese Rotarians what it means to perceive space and time as a Westerner: "Every aspect of Western life assert[s] with untiring iteration the *exclusive integrity* of things, objects. . . . The spaces between objects . . . are not perceived actually as integers at all. . . ."

I have taken this long excursion into other cultures to show how in these, free time, through being recognized as valid existence, can and does contain value. In our own culture it is perceived as the unallocated, the unscheduled, the nothing; and it cannot contain value, as it contains no being. In the minds of many who despair over juvenile delinquency, alcoholism and other social ills, it is regarded as the vacuum which (Western) Nature abhors. Why then have we in this country taken such a good word, a word which names our valued way of life, and applied it to an emptiness? Do we recognize only a freedom *from?*

I cannot answer the first question except upon the basis of speculation. I believe that freedom *from,* the condition of the situation, was at one time felt to be supremely necessary but has since been taken for granted. And, with the increasing emphasis on the individual, on the *self* as a focus and starting point, the *situation* has lost significance. The individual is no longer supremely interested in *what can be done,* but rather in *what I can do.* When Papashvily came from Russian Georgia to this country, he saw it as the land where Anything Can Happen. But when I came to the land of the free as a foreign student in the mid-twenties, my classmates were not phrasing it in that way; they sang: "*I can do anything, anything, anything.*" Freedom is now expressed as capacity, as ability residing in the self; perhaps earned by the self through the acquisition of know-how or through training but not necessarily so. We do recognize a freedom *to*, but we do not refer to it in this way. To be free is vague, conditional and not the main point; what is vital is that I *can*. Our school teachers are fighting a losing battle when they try to teach their pupils to ask, "May I?" The *can*, emanating from the self, subsumes all other nuances of freedom; and after all, even if I am not "allowed to," I can still take matters in my own hands.

The *can*, nevertheless, refers to a personal capacity only. The emphasis has shifted from a passive potentiality in the situation to a vital capacity in the person. Yet this ability still has to be actualized, to be translated into doing or functioning. The situation may allow; the parents, the teachers, the supervisor may permit; but this is not enough. At one time leaders in the field of interpersonal relations held that unlimited freedom *from* would be conducive to freedom *for* or *to*. But recently this notion has been questioned. Educational leaders now consider that unbounded freedom is chaotic and frightening, and they advocate the setting of limits. But the limit, in American imagery, is something external; so we have seen the suggested limit as a surrounding boundary, a fence around the formless area of freedom.

But I believe that the trouble is not that the individual is frightened by unbounded freedom, but rather that the lack of structure leaves him inert. And the introduction of outer boundaries is no solution, within the American cultural framework. What incites the American individual to an answering engagement in the situation is definiteness, caliber, *within* the situation; a strong framework, "guts." Unstructured freedom, whether fenced in or not, is still namby-pamby. The limits must have the character of a skeleton. Randomness, the unplanned and unscheduled, are like the despised jellyfish, and perpetuate or evoke inertia. Modupe's silences, during which he became attuned to the rhythm of the earth, do not incite to an answering actualization of the capacity to do or feel.

This is why American leisure has to be filled with named games, organized recreation, labelled hobbies, planned activities. And this is why the *have to* is often paradoxically freeing.

There are questions raised beyond this: Does this version of freedom, with its dependence on the pre-planned and its main emphasis on the capacity of the self, engender creativity, originality, spontaneity? My own opinion is that it does not; that indefiniteness and randomness, the recognition of the pauses, are all essential to creativity. There is the further question as to whether capacity is automatically transformed into actualization, the *can* into *I do*, even in the presence of the structured. I answer this in terms of the American philosophy of the self as expressed, for example, in client-centered therapy: that the individual has to be enabled, and the function of the loving mother, of the trusting and trusted social environment, is to enable. And when enabling is present, it can also break through the meager confines of the American version of freedom, into the unsheltered spaces in between the defined projects and planned activities. But the discussion of these questions is beyond the scope of this article.

REFERENCES

Riesman, David. "The Suburban Dislocation" in *Metropolis in Ferment.* THE ANNALS of the American Academy of Political and Social Science. Vol. 314, November, 1957.

Lee, Dorothy. "Freedom, Spontaneity and Limit in American Linguistic Usage" *Explorations 4,* 1955.

Prince Modupe. *I Was a Savage.* Harcourt, Brace and Co., New York, 1957.

Standing Bear, Luther. *My People the Sioux.* Boston: Houghton Mifflin Co., 1928.

————. *Land of the Spotted Eagle.* Boston: Houghton Mifflin Co., 1932.

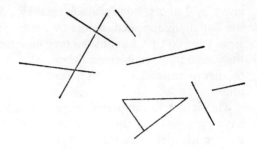

Responsibility

among the Dakota

THE QUESTION OF RESPONSIBILITY was raised when Cain retorted: "Am I my brother's keeper?" Throughout the years, it has been the concern of religion, ethics, law, social science. We ask: To what extent is an individual responsible for others? Who determines this responsibility? What gives rise to the responsibility? action and its consequences? the mere fact of being? Is responsibility equated with accountability? What is a man's responsibility as a representative? Is it his responsibility to carry out majority decision when he differs from the majority?

To help find answers to these questions, I went to the study of a society radically different from ours; so different that much of what I say may appear at first sight to be irrelevant to what we call responsibility. The culture I studied was that of the Dakota, as it existed in the eighteen-seventies.

I have chosen this society because I was impressed by the sense of responsibility accompanying behavior. Yet, the areas of behavior and experience I describe here may not be the ones which we would select to describe when speaking of our own culture, because to choose according

Paper presented to the Faculty Seminar on Individual Liberty and Social Responsibility of the Institute of Religious and Social Studies, 1957-1958.

to my own cultural framework, would have meant to lose what is fresh and new for us in the culture of the Dakota. I have used only accounts given by Dakota, largely autobiographic, dealing with the period before the buffalo disappeared, before they were forbidden to perform their religious rites; so that I could discover how the Dakota themselves saw their function and place in the universe, what they considered to be their duty to themselves and to society, how they envisioned their relationship to others.

This is not the impartial picture which a trained ethnographer would have presented had there been one to observe them at that early date. It gives much that is always absent from the ethnographic description and it omits the outsider's view and interpretation. Naturally their own view of themselves is different from that of their White conquerors. It is no secret that the White Americans, the army of the time, the government, the White settlers and the prospectors in the Black Hills, saw the Dakota in general as murderous and treacherous, and called them the "Fighting Sioux." But the men whose autobiographies I read saw themselves as people who were related to every part and aspect of the universe, and whose deepest concern was to experience, understand, and enhance this universal relatedness at the cost of hardship, privation, and great pain; whose ideal was peace and harmony with all. To what extent this ideal was at all realized before the coming of the Whites who, in the eyes of the Dakota, hunted them and tried to exterminate them as they did their brother the buffalo we do not know; we do know from their autobiographies that they had traditional "enemies," and that to go on the warpath against these was honorable, an exercise of their manly properties, a validation of their sacred power.

The warfare of the Dakota was not motivated by hatred of their enemies. "I looked upon them," says Eastman, "more as the college athlete regards his rivals from another college. There was no thought of destroying a nation, taking away their country and reducing the people to servitude, for my race earlier honored and bestowed gifts upon their enemies at the next meeting." He refers to the Utes as "our bravest enemies." If the Dakota perpetrated unspeakable cruelties upon them, this was no more than what they expected to meet themselves with fortitude, and in fact voluntarily submitted themselves to, during certain ritual occasions.

The Whites, at any rate, eventually enforced peace upon them; but in trying to subjugate their fighting spirit, they also forbade them to perform the rites which were basic to the experiencing of universal relatedness; and when this went, the unquestioned responsibility which arose from the feeling of relatedness, disappeared also.

II

The Dakota were responsible for all things, because they were at one with all things. In one way, this meant that all behavior had to be responsible, since its effect always went beyond the individual. In another way, it meant that an individual had to, was responsible to, increase, intensify, spread, recognize, experience this relationship. To grow in manliness, in humanness, in holiness, meant to plunge purposively deeper into the relatedness of all things. A Dakota never *assumed* responsibility, because responsibility was had, was there always. Where we would say that a man *assumed* a new responsibility, they would consider that, in such a situation, a man made an autonomous decision to carry out this particular *had* responsibility; or perhaps, that at the moment he was able to recognize this responsibility, or to act responsibly. For the Dakota, to be was to be responsible; because to be was to be related; and to be related meant to be responsible.

It remained for the Dakota to recognize his relatedness, and his responsibility; it was there for him to discover. Growth meant increase in responsibility only in that it meant increasing recognition of the responsibility of being Dakota, being human, and being a part of the universe. Growth did not come automatically. Children had to be brought up in awareness of their relatedness, in the exercise of responsibility and increasingly of autonomous responsibility. They had to learn that they were responsible to enhance and intensify their recognition of relatedness and their very relatedness.

The bringing up of Dakota children was such that they grew up to feel that they were part of nature, or relatives of all things, to feel that "there was no complete solitude," because, wherever they were, they were with their relatives—the rocks, the trees, the wind. They grew to feel, as Standing Bear put it, ". . . that we are of the soil and the soil is of us. We love the birds and beasts that grew with us on this soil. They drank the same water and breathed the same air. We are all one in nature." Responsibility toward the buffalo, reluctance to kill wantonly, to waste any of the products of nature, stemmed from this feeling of relatedness and mutuality. "I was only a part of everything that was called the world," recalled Standing Bear. "I can now see that humaneness is not a thing that can be ordered by law."

When the Dakota sat on the ground, they sat on the lap of their mother Earth. In the winter, they bathed their bodies in the sunshine as they did in the icy water of the streams; or they stripped themselves to go out into the rainstorm, "to be alone with Rain," because they felt "a unity with these tremendous forces." Their bodies were nourished by rain and sun and wind just as much as by meat and plant food. The growing child was taught to be sensitive and highly perceptive of all natural phenomena —of wind and insects and plants—so that he could receive instruction from them, knowledge and guidance and advice. "There was no such thing as emptiness in the world . . . Everywhere there was life, visible and invisible, and every object possessed something that would be good for us to have also—even to the very stones. The world teemed with life and wisdom." "The approach of the Indian toward the animal kingdom was not in the manner of a detached study but more the natural process of 'getting acquainted'—an exchange of friendship."

The corollary of this postulate of relatedness, even of oneness, with the universe, was that the self was, or became eventually, co-extensive with the universe. A man recalls that his father taught him that to serve his tribe was to serve himself. To fail in one's duty to others, meant to fail in a test of manhood. Conversely, a boy had the duty to develop himself, to increase in hardihood, in physical prowess, in skill, in bravery, because through enhancing himself he enhanced his society. The co-extensiveness of self and society was brought home to the individual by the practice of having the reward of achievement go to others. When Standing Bear as a boy of about five killed his first bird, his father celebrated the event by giving away a horse to someone else, an old man who could never return the gift. "This was the beginning of my religious training," remarks Standing Bear. When a group of older boys to whom he had attached himself killed a deer, they gave him a portion as his due for being present at the kill, and his father again gave away a gift of a horse; individual achievement is completely obliterated here. Since the self is not distinguished, gratitude has no part in the picture; so that when a warrior gave a horse to the village crier for an orphan boy, he neither expected nor received thanks; on the other hand, a group of his village-mates formed a band to sing his praises.

From the time a child could walk, he was encouraged to give to others. When mothers were giving to the weak and old, they gave portions to their children also, so that they could give their own gifts to those in need. The good man, the "man whom all praise," was the man who trained himself rigorously in responsibility. He was one who never broke laws, who was always generous and saw to it that the needy had meat, who was good to everybody in the band. When he was selected to be a "man whom all praise" he vowed to belong, not to himself, but to the people.

To enhance relatedness, to pierce deeper into the mystery of universal oneness and experience the ultimate unity of all, a Dakota had to go through one or more rites, approaching the ultimate in absolute humility and complete abandonment of self. Men and women would undergo the Rite of Purification "for all the people of the world that they may see clearly in walking the *wakan* path; that they may know all that is holy, and that they may increase in a sacred manner." The fragrance of the sweet grass they burned during the rite was to "make the four-leggeds, the wingeds, the star peoples of the heavens and all things as relatives." When a boy was "just beginning to be a man" he had to go on a vision quest. This involved a long, complex rite, beginning with purification.

During a deeply religious ceremonial, the holy man who sponsored the lamenter filled a sacred pipe, systematically putting into it every part and aspect of the universe. On behalf of the lamenter he prayed: "O You four Powers of the universe, you wingeds of the air, and all the peoples who move in the universe—you have all been placed in the pipe . . . O *Wakan-Tanka*, grant that this young man may have relatives; that he may be one with the four winds, the four Powers of the world, and with the light of the dawn. May he understand his relationship with all the winged peoples of the air." "Our Grandmother and Mother (earth) . . . this young man wishes to become one with all things . . . For the good of all your peoples, help him!" Eventually, the lamenter climbed to a selected spot on a mountain, where alone, exposed to the elements, without defense against the constant danger of lurking enemies, without shelter, naked and fasting, walking in a sacred manner within the sacred circle prepared for him, emptied of self, straining to penetrate beyond the senses, he prayed continually, "O *Wakan-Tanka*, have pity on me, that my people may live!" It was a sacred responsibility to lament for the vision, because, says Black Elk, "It helps us realize our oneness with all things, to know that all things are our relatives; and then on behalf of all things we pray to *Wakan-Tanka* . . ." When the lamenter prayed with the sacred pipe, he prayed "for and with everything."

The most intense experience of relatedness, and the deepest sense of common responsibility, came when the lamenting was done during the Sun-dance, when a man participated with others who had similarly vowed to "offer my body and soul that my people may live . . . ," while relatives and friends supported them with their presence and ministrations. At this time, the dancers underwent agonizing pain, offering flesh and blood to the Sun, praying: "In tears and suffering I shall hold my pipe and raise my voice to You, O *Wakan-Tanka* . . . May we take upon ourselves much of the suffering of the people." Eventually, these men could say: "Behold me . . . for I represent the people . . . ," and: "I am the people."

Responsibility was rooted in this increasing awareness of relationship, but was not identical with it. In the experiences which were open to the Dakota child, responsibility was an ever-present dimension. The child was given responsible work, with social results. When he was about three, Standing Bear would be sent to bring his father's pony to be bridled, and to get the village whetstone—a difficult task, as he had to go from tipi to tipi until he found it. With this came the development of autonomy: there was no supervision; the child was trusted to carry out his responsibility. No external inducement was offered; and in fact, "no one ever said to a child, 'Do this and I will pay you for it.'" Neither was coercion used in teaching responsible behavior. "Father . . . never said, 'You have to do this,' or 'You must do that.' But when doing things himself he would often say something like 'Son, some day when you are a man you will do this.'"

Coercion and persuasion were not acceptable among the Dakota since no man could decide for another, nor was responsible for the behavior of another. Ideally, at any rate, orders were not given to anyone. Decisions were all autonomous, except during the buffalo hunt and warfare, when the group had to act in concert. In moving camp, every family had its place in the line, no one had the need to be ahead of the others, so that, though several hundred people might be moving, there was no confusion and no one directing operations. The council made no laws that were enforceable on others; it made decisions. So that, if it were decided to move camp, a family or two might elect to stay in the old site, without interference.

It is true that Dakota writers speak of the obligation of the child to obey, and of "lessons in obedience." Yet the very same writers speak of a "following the father's advice" rather than obeying a command, and show how repeatedly they chose autonomously what would please their father, rather than doing what he ordered them to do. The respect and approval of the older generation as well as of the band in general was perhaps a strong incentive in responsible behavior. Fathers said to their sons, "Thus will the tribe think well of you" and "You must be pure and honorable so that people will respect you." Yet there was also satisfaction in acting honorably, generously, responsibly, with fortitude, whether it was known and approved or not. Boys in school in the East acted in a way that would please fathers who never knew about it. And to act in autonomous responsibility, rather than in obedience to command, was in itself good and admirable.

Autonomy was a prerogative of all, young and old, men and women. Children learned early to act at their own decision. By the age of seven, Standing Bear was acting responsibly without suggestion from others. When the cry was raised that the enemy was about while he was playing with his sisters far from home, he waited in great fear until he saw his sisters safely home before he whipped his pony to leave the spot. When he was eleven, some Whites came to recruit students for Carlisle, the new school which was being opened in Pennsylvania for Indian children. Standing Bear saw this as an opportunity for showing bravery by moving into the camp of the enemy, and rendered his application. The White visitors, however, would not accept the decision of a small boy, without having the father's consent. In the end, the father came only as a matter of form, endorsing the son's decision only to comply with the strange request of the Whites. He did not think it was up to him to give his permission; rather, it was up to his son to make his own decision, about his own life. It was a tenet of the society that no man could decide for another. So Crazy Horse, when presented with the pipe of peace by mediating chiefs, said, "Ask my people what they wish to do." "Each person could be as truthful, as honest, as industrious, or as brave as he wished— could even go to battle upon his own initiative." The Dakota had contempt for the White soldier, "who required another man to tell him to pick up his gun, to stand, run, halt, salute, and march into the foe."

The Dakota were responsible, but were accountable to no one for their conduct. Responsibility and accountability had nothing in common for them. Ideally, everyone was responsible for all members of the band, and eventually for all people, all things. It was the duty of everyone to see to it that "the right of every person to eat and be clothed was respected, and there was no more question about it than there was about the free and ungoverned use of sunshine, pure air, and the rain which bathed our bodies . . ." Yet, no Dakota was accountable to any one or for any one. Was he his brother's keeper? Yes, in so far as he was responsible for his welfare; no, in so far as being accountable for him. He would never speak for him, decide for him, answer prying questions about him. And he was not accountable for himself, either. No one asked him questions about himself; he gave information or withheld it, at his own choice. When a man came back from the vision quest, when warriors returned, they were not questioned. People waited for them to report or not as they pleased.

Autonomy and non-accountability could be maintained only through absolute trust in the other. Autonomy was possible because the individual was trusted to behave responsibly. As there was no supervision of the child, so there was no overseer for the adult, no checking. During a buffalo hunt, the welfare of the entire group depended on the word of the scout; yet he was not cross-questioned, not asked for corroboration or verification. So a warrior was believed when he reported his exploits and he did not have to bring back a trophy by way of proof.

There is a further responsibility for the Dakota, which I have not made explicit yet. It is implied, however, in much of what I have said. It is indicated in a man's duty to seek a vision, for example. To see a vision, sought or unsought, to receive sacred power, meant to be responsible to actualize the dream, to realize the potentiality. Black Elk had an unsought vision when he was a boy of nine; and he felt deeply and in the end despairingly the responsibility to reproduce his vision in worldly terms.

These are only pointed instances, however, of the responsibility which permeated all being: the responsibility to actualize ultimate reality. Black Elk speaks of the great happiness he felt when he finally performed his vision at the age of seventeen and of how in the midst of the performance he saw, in the cloud above, the timeless reality which he was bringing into history; and he "knew the real was yonder, and the darkened dream of it was here."

This ultimate reality was beyond existence; it was like the script of a play, waiting to be staged and acted. It was timeless and limitless, without substance, waiting for man to give it body, the here and now. The visible, knowable world was its reflection, a temporary manifestation which could not deplete the infinite reality. In this reality, all was one; everything: all animals and plants, the heavenly bodies, the rocks, the earth, the sky, the cardinal directions; here the one was many and the many one. "It is only the ignorant person that sees many where there is really only one," said Black Elk.

To actualize this, to act out a play that was true and good, a man had to become aware of the truth of this relatedness, this oneness; to experience it in its ultimate truth. Parents could help their children only to recognize the manifest, the phenomenal. It was to make himself capable of fulfilling his responsibility to actualize that a Dakota sought a vision. He actualized what already was: it was not his responsibility to create. He gave form to the vision which was granted to him, which came to him; he did not select. But he was an autonomous agent. At his own decision he requested help of a holy man who had plunged deep into reality. At his own initiative he finally stood alone in bodily pain, in suffering, in supplication, yet with dignity, making the supreme effort to enter into the experience with ultimate reality. He stood in humility, because he knew that "man did not occupy a special place in the eyes of *Wakan*." Yet, "he was humble without cringing, without loss of spirit. He always faced the Powers in prayer; he never grovelled on the earth, but with face lifted to the sky he spoke straight to his Mystery." Without *Wakan* he was weak and ineffective, yet he was a free, an autonomous agent without whom *Wakan* could find no actualization.

And in doing this, he was simultaneously fulfilling a responsibility to his people. Whatever his prayer, the theme which is repeated is "Be merciful to me, that my people may live."

Not all men could plunge equally deeply into the ultimate, and many were not able to obtain a vision. No women went on a vision quest. On rare occasions, a boy refused to go on a quest, choosing to remain unmanly, or even to be classed with women. Sometimes a boy would run back home in fear, after his first night's vigil; and at times the only thing that kept him on his mountain was the knowledge that if he ran back home he could never go on a vision quest again, he would never have the opportunity to get power from *Wakan Tanka*.

Is this to say that some people were more responsible than others? I would say that, ideally, all behaved responsibly, but that as relatedness was felt and understood more deeply the sense of responsibility deepened. A man like Crazy Horse was felt to be always acting for the sake of his people, as representative of his people, perhaps in identity with his people; he was considered selfless, a holy man—so holy, that the Dakota felt that he finally could be killed only because he was taken unawares. Black Elk began by feeling responsible for all his people, and as he matured, his responsibility became more compelling and more extensive, until, in the end, he dictated to a White a description of the Seven Sacred Rites of the Dakota, because it was imperative that the knowledge be handed down and there was no Dakota capable of taking and retaining it. He dictated it "Through no other desire than to help my people in understanding the greatness and truth of our tradition, *and also to help in bringing peace upon the earth, not only among men, but within men, and between the whole of creation.*" (italics mine).

III

I return now to the questions which I posed in the beginning of this essay:

Wherein lies the responsibility of the Dakota? Primarily, I believe it derives from being—being a member of a family, or a specific camp circle; being Dakota, being human, and being part of the universe. Not all parts of the universal whole carry the same responsibility. It is the responsibility of the four-leggeds to furnish food for the two-leggeds, for example; this was determined in the beginning, before beings were differentiated into four-leggeds and two-leggeds. As I understand it, it is the responsibility of man alone to actualize the universe; it is his unique role. Whether it is the White man's role, I do not know; it certainly is the responsibility of all the Dakota bands. There is the specific responsibility to one's own camp circle, to one's companions on the warpath, to one's family. Perhaps we might say that a man's responsibility to wife and parents-in-law arose as a consequence of an autonomous act of marriage. But I believe that eventually it is being a husband or a son-in-law, just as being a brother or a son, which is the basis of the responsibility.

Who determines responsibility? Generally speaking, child-rearing and education consisted in pointing out to the growing individual the basis, the extent, the kind of responsibility. Parents and other immediate relatives were the guides and sponsors in the beginning, but after adolescence, the boy, the man, on his own accord turned to the known wise and holy men of the band for further guidance. Yet, no one determined responsibility for someone else. The individual, instructed and guided, determined it for himself.

Next comes the question as to representation: is there a conflict between a man's private responsibility and his responsibility as a representative of a group? I believe that seen against the Dakota situation this question is nonsense; because representation there was something different from the conception of representation which makes it possible for me to ask this question. For the Dakota, ultimately or at any rate ideally, the man who said "I represent the people" could also say "I am the people." Yet this does not mean that, in representing the people, I can come to decisions affecting others, or that others have delegated to me the right to speak for them. It means that when I suffer in supplication, my people are suffering through me, when I am enhanced and strengthened, my people are enhanced in me, when I see the light of truth, my people see the truth, because I am the people.

The council itself of the Dakota, was not representative in my understanding of the term. It was composed of men who were mature, men of experience, wisdom and prestige, who discussed matters pertaining to the welfare of the group, helped clarify the obscure, settled disputes and generally furnished guidance for the group. Their decisions were announced to the group but not enforced upon the group, except for the communal buffalo hunt. The buffalo was basic to the survival of the Dakota. It furnished their food, their tipis, their clothing, many of their utensils and ceremonial instruments. For anyone to act on his own intitiative or independently during the hunt might mean to endanger the welfare of the entire group. Under these circumstances, the soldier-society undertook to enforce the decision of the council, on pain of serious punishment.

The council of the Dakota could not speak for the people. Whether it conveyed a majority decision or not is not the point here, because the will of the majority was irrelevant in the worldview of the Dakota; and some of the difficulty between the Whites and the Dakota, as, for example, over the ceding of the Black Hills, came out of the different views held as to majority decision and representation by Whites and Indians. For the Dakota the end of discussion in council was to reach agreement, not as to expediency, not as to the preferable, but as to the only right course. There was no conflict of responsibility here.

REFERENCES

Black Elk Speaks. Being the Life Story of a Holy Man of the Oglala Sioux, as told to John G. Neihardt (Flaming Rainbow). New York: William Morrow & Company, 1932.

Brown, Joseph Epes *The Sacred Pipe, Black Elk's Account of the Seven Rites of the Oglala Sioux.* Recorded and edited by Joseph Epes Brown. Norman: University of Oklahoma Press, 1953.

Eastman, Charles A. (Ohiyesa) *An Indian Boyhood.* Boston: Little, Brown & Company, 1902.

————. *Old Indian Days.* Boston: Little, Brown & Company, 1907.

————. *From the Deep Woods to Civilization; Chapters in the Autobiography of an Indian.* Boston: Little, Brown & Company, 1916.

————. *Indian Heroes and Great Chieftains.* Boston: Little, Brown & Company, 1918.

Neihardt, John G. *When the Tree Flowered; An Authentic Tale of the Old Sioux World.* New York: Macmillan Company, 1951.

Olden, Sarah Emilia. *The People of Tipi Sapa.* Milwaukee: Morehouse Publishing Company, 1918.

Standing Bear, Luther. *My People the Sioux.* Boston: Houghton Mifflin Company, 1928.

————. *Land of the Spotted Eagle.* Boston: Houghton Mifflin Company, 1932.

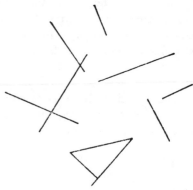

Are Basic Needs Ultimate?

THE PURPOSE OF THIS PAPER IS TO URGE a re-examination of the premise which so many of us implicitly hold that culture is a group of patterned means for the satisfaction of a list of human needs. This is, of course, not a new issue either with psychologists or anthropologists. The concept of an inventory of basic needs rose to fill the vacuum created when the behaviorists banished the old list of instincts. Yet, in spite of dissatisfaction with this, many of us continue to think of cultural behavior in terms of some form of the stimulus-response principle. Anthropologists borrowed the principle from psychology, without first testing it against ethnographic material, so that often, when the psychologist uses anthropological material, he gets his own back again in new form, and receives no new insights. There are two assumptions involved here: (1) the premise that action occurs in answer to a need or a lack; and (2) the premise that there is a list. In recent years, anthropologists, influenced by the new psychology, have often substituted *drives* or *impulses* or *adjustive responses* for the old term *needs*, but the concept of the list remains with us. We hold this side by side with the conflicting conception of culture as a totality, of personality as organismic, as well as

From *Journal of Abnormal and Social Psychology*, 1948, Vol. 43.

with adherence to psychosomatic principles. We deplore the presentation of culture as a list of traits, yet we are ready to define culture as an answer to a list of needs.

This definition of culture has proved a strain. When we found that the original list of basic needs or drives was inadequate, we, like the psychologists, tried to solve the difficulty by adding on a list of social and psychic needs; and, from here on, I use the term *need* in a broad sense, to cover the stimulus-response phrasing of behavior. When the list proved faulty, all we had to do was to add to the list. We have now such needs as that for novelty, for escape from reality, for security, for emotional response. We have primary needs, or drives, and secondary needs, and we have secondary needs playing the role of primary needs. The endless process of adding and correcting is not an adequate improvement; neither does the occasional substitution of a "totality of needs" for a "list of needs" get at the root of the trouble. Where so much elaboration and revision is necessary, I suspect that the original unit itself must be at fault; we must have a radical change.

In applying the list of needs to different cultures, we found that modification was necessary. It was apparent that the need for food of a member of American society is far greater than that of the members of most other societies. Curiously enough, we also find that though a laborer on a New Guinea plantation needs a minimum diet of seven pounds of yams, plus a stated amount of meat, an Arapesh in his own hamlet, working in his fields, climbing up and down steep mountain sides, working hard at ceremonials, can live a meaningful life and procreate healthy children on three pounds of yams a day, and almost no meat.

Is further modification necessary here, or is there another factor at work? Faced with data of this sort, we have been tempted to apply a utilitarian calculus. We have said that when the Arapesh gardens inefficiently in company with his brother-in-law, and when he plants his fruit tree on someone else's distant land, he multiplies his exertions and minimizes his subsistence so as to achieve a maximum of social warmth. But is he really filling two distinct needs, slighting one at the expense of the other? When he takes his pig to another hamlet, and asks someone else's wife to feed and bring it up, what need exactly is he satisfying? And is this need greater than the general human need for food? And does its satisfaction supply a substitute for caloric intake? These questions are nonsense, but we do run into them if we carry the premise of a list of needs far enough.

The assumption of a list of needs was put under its greatest strain, I think, during the recent war. We had assumed that "the role of . . .

needs in human behavior is that of first causes." Then how could we explain the behavior of certain small nations, who chose freely to lose necessary food, shelter, security, etc., rather than join the Axis? Why did whole nations court physical annihilation rather than subscribe to Axis doctrines? Why did fathers and husbands and daughters expose their beloved families to danger of torture or death by joining the underground? In this country, why did millions of people who had adequate food and shelter and "security" choose to jeopardize their lives? We can say, of course, that they were satisfying their need for emotional response, in this case the approval of others. One anthropologist did express it in this way. But why was it this particular course of action which was sure to bring them the approval of others? And how could these needs have been the cause of behavior whose goal was neither individual nor group survival?

To my mind, this means that either needs are not the cause of all behavior, or that the list of needs provides an inadequate unit for assessing human behavior. I am not saying that there are no needs; rather, that if there are needs, they are derivative not basic. If, for example, physical survival was held as the ultimate goal in some society, it would probably be found to give rise to those needs which have been stated to be basic to human survival; but I know of no culture where human physical survival has been shown, rather than unquestioningly assumed by social scientists, to be the ultimate goal.

I believe that it is value, not a series of needs, which is at the basis of human behavior. The main difference between the two lies in the conception of the good which underlies them. The premise that man acts so as to satisfy needs presupposes a negative conception of the good as amelioration or the correction of an undesirable state. According to this view, man acts to relieve tension; good is the removal of evil and welfare the correction of ills; satisfaction is the meeting of a need; good functioning comes from adjustment, survival from adaptation; peace is the resolution of conflict; fear, of the supernatural or of adverse public opinion, is the incentive to good conduct; the happy individual is the well-adjusted individual.

Perhaps this view of what constitutes the good is natural and applicable in a culture which also holds that man was born in sin, whether in Biblical or in psychoanalytic terms. But should we, who believe that other cultures should be assessed according to their own categories and premises, impose upon them our own unexamined conception of the good, and thus always see them as striving to remove or avoid ills? It seems to me that, when we do not take this negative view of the good for granted, other cultures often appear to be maintaining "justment" rather than striving to attain adjustment. For example, for the Hopi, the good is present and positive. An individual is "born in hopiness," so to speak, and strives throughout life to maintain and enhance this hopiness. There is no external reward for being good, as this is taken for granted. It is evil which is external and intrusive, making a man kahopi, or unhopi; that is, un-peaceful, ungood.

In my opinion, the motivation underlying Hopi behavior is *value*. To the Hopi, there is value in acting as a Hopi within a Hopi situation; there is satisfaction in the situation itself, not in the solution of it or the resolution of tension. I speak of value, but rather than define it I shall indicate what I mean by presenting value situations. I want to point out that the notion of value is incompatible with that of a list of needs, or adjustive responses, or drives; so that, wherever it is held, the list must go.

Now, if we substitute the notion of value for that of needs, we are no longer troubled with the difficulty of trying to assess a totality in terms of an aggregate, since value is total and is to be found in a total situation. When we listen to a symphony, we get satisfaction from a whole, not from eighteen thousand notes and a series of arrangements. I can give you an inventory of my daughter, her three teeth, her seventeen pounds, her inability to sit up yet, her mixed smell, her bald head; is it this which causes my behavior when I rush joyfully home to her as soon as I leave my office?

Again, we find that the Hopi like to eat corn; would we be justified in assuming that a Hopi would therefore find it good to work for wages so as to earn money to buy corn to satisfy his hunger? To the Hopi, corn is not nutrition; it is a totality, a way of life. Something of this sort is exemplified in the story which Talayesva tells of the Mexican trader who offered to sell salt to the Hopi group who were starting out on a highly ceremonial Salt Expedition. Within its context this offer to relieve the group of the hardships and dangers of the religious journey sounds ridiculous. The Hopi were not just going to get salt to season their dishes. To them, the journey was part of the process of growing corn and of maintaining harmonious interrelations with nature and what we call the divine. It was the Hopi Way, containing Hopi value. Yet even an ethnographer, dealing with Hopi culture in terms of basic needs, views the Salt Expedition as the trader did, and classifies it under *Secondary Economic Activities.*

So also with our earlier example of the Arapesh. Their eating is not a distinct act satisfying a single need. Food to the Arapesh is good; it incorporates intensive social intercourse; it is the medium of intimacy and identification with others, the symbol of human relations which to them are the primary good. It satisfies the total individual. When we analyze the mouthful of yams into so much nutrition plus so much social warmth, that is exactly what we are doing and no more; we do not find these distinctions or elements—we create them. What we find are aspects of a total situation without independent existence. Our impulse is to break up the situation because we are culturally trained to comprehend a totality only after we break it up into familiar phrasings. But in this way we miss the value inherent in it, since it disappears with analysis, and cannot be recreated synthetically afterwards. Having created a series of elements, we then find no difficulty in motivating them according to a series of needs.

If needs are inborn and discrete, we should find them as such in the earliest situations of an individual's life. Yet take the Tikopia or the Kwoma infant, held and suckled without demand in the mother's encircling arms. He knows no food apart from society, has no need for emotional response since his society is emotionally continuous with himself; he certainly feels no need for security. He participates in a total situation. Even in our own culture, the rare happy child has no need for emotional response or approval or security or escape from reality or novelty. If we say that the reason that he has no need for these things is that he does have them already, we would be begging the question. I believe, rather, that these terms or notions are irrelevant when satisfaction is viewed in terms of positive present value, and value itself as inherent in a total situation.

On the other hand, it is possible to see needs as arising out of the basic value of a culture. In our own culture, the value of individualism is axiomatically assumed. How else would it be possible for us to pluck twenty infants, newly severed from complete unity with their mothers, out of all social and emotional context, and classify them as twenty atoms on the basis of a similarity of age? On this assumption of individualism, a mother has need for individual self-expression. She has to have time for and by herself; and since she values individualism, the mother in our culture usually does have this need for a private life.

We also believe that a newborn infant must become individuated, must be taught physical and emotional self-dependence; we assume, in fact, that he has a separate identity which he must be helped to recognize. We believe that he has distinct rights, and sociologists urge us to reconcile the needs of the child to those of the adults in the family, on the assumption, of course, that needs and ends are individual, not social. Now, in maintaining our individual integrity and in passing on our value of individualism to the infant, we create needs for food, for security, for emotional response, phrasing these as distinct and separate. We force the infant to go hungry, and we see suckling as merely a matter of nutrition, so that we can then feel free to substitute a bottle for the breast and a mechanical bottle-holder for the mother's arms; thus we ensure privacy for the mother and teach the child self-dependence. We create needs in the infant by withholding affection and then presenting it as a series of approvals for an inventory of achievements or attributes. On the assumption that there is no emotional continuum, we withdraw ourselves, thus forcing the child to strive for emotional response and security. And thus, though habituation and teaching, the mother reproduces in the child her own needs, in this case the need for privacy which inevitably brings with it related needs.

Now the child grows up needing time to himself, a room of his own, freedom of choice, freedom to plan his own time and his own life. He will brook no interference and no encroachment. He will spend his wealth installing private bathrooms in his house, buying a private car, a private yacht, private woods and a private beach, which he will then people with his privately chosen society. The need for privacy is an imperative one in our society, recognized by official bodies of our government. And it is part of a system which stems from and expresses our basic value.

In other cultures, we find other systems, maintaining other values. The Arapesh, with their value of the social, created a wide gap between ownership and possession, which they could then bridge with a multitude of human relations. They plant their trees in some one else's hamlet, they rear pigs owned by someone else, they eat yams planted by someone else. The Ontong-Javanese, for whom also the good is social, value the sharing of the details of everyday living. They have created a system, very confusing to an American student, whereby a man is a member of at least three ownership groups, determined along different principles, which are engaged cooperatively in productive activities; and of two large households, one determined along matrilineal lines, one along patrilineal lines. Thus, an Ontong-Javanese man spends part of the year with his wife's sisters and their families, sharing with them the intimate details of daily life, and the rest of the year on an outlying island, with his brothers and their families. The poor man is the man who has no share in an outlying island, who must eat and sleep only in a household composed of his immediate family and his mother's kin, when unmarried; and who must spend the whole year with his wife's kin, when married. He has the same amount and kind of food to eat as his wealthy neighbors, but not as many coco-nuts to give away; he has shelter as adequate as that of the wealthy, but not as much of the shared living which is the Ontong-Javanese good.

In speaking of these other cultures, I have not used the term *need*. I could have said, for example, that the Ontong-Javanese needs a large house, to include many maternally related families. But I think this would have been merely an exercise in analysis. On the other hand, when I spoke of our own culture, I was forced to do it in terms of needs, since I have been trained to categorize my own experience in these terms. But even here, these are not basic needs, but rather part of a system expressing our basic value; and were we able to break away from our substantival or formal basis of categorizing, I think we should find these to be aspects or stresses or functions, without independent existence. Culture is not, I think, "a response to the total needs of a society"; but rather a system which stems from and expresses something had, the basic values of society.

REFERENCES

Allport, Gordon *Personality.* New York: H. Holt & Company, 1937.

Beaglehole, E. *Notes on Hopi Economic Life.* Yale University Publications in An-thropology, no. 15. New Haven: Yale University Press, 1937.

Firth, Raymond *We, The Tikopia.* New York: American Book Company, 1936.

Gillin, J. "Cultural Adjustment." *American Anthropology,* 46:429-447 (1944).

Hogbin, I. *Law and Order in Polynesia.* New York: Harcourt, Brace and Company, Inc., 1934.

Kardiner, A. *The Individual and His Society.* New York: Columbia University Press, 1939.

Kluckhohn, Clyde and W. H. Kelly "The Concept of Culture." In Linton, R. (ed.) *The Science of Man in the World Crisis.* New York: Columbia University Press, 1945.

Lewin, K. *A Dynamic Theory of Personality.* New York: McGraw-Hill Book Company, 1935.

Linton, R. *The Study of Man.* New York: D. Appleton-Century Company, Inc., 1936.

————. *The Cultural Basis of Personality.* New York: D. Appleton-Century Com-pany, Inc., 1945.

Mead, Margaret *Sex and Temperament in Three Primitive Societies.* New York: William Morrow & Company, Inc., 1935.

————. "The Arapesh of New Guinea." In Mead, M. (ed.) *Cooperation and Competition Among Primitive Peoples.* New York: McGraw-Hill Book Company, 1937.

————. *The Mountain Arapesh: I. An Importing Culture.* Anthropological Papers of the American Museum of Natural History, 36: pt. 3 (1938).

Murdock. G. P. "The Science of Culture." *American Anthropology,* 34:200-215 (1932).

Murray, H. A. *Explorations in Personality.* New York: Oxford University Press, 1938.

Parsons, E. C. (ed.) *A Pueblo Indian Journal, 1920-1921.* (American Anthropological Association Memoirs, no. 32.) Menasha, Wisconsin, 1925.

Simmons, Leo W. *Sun Chief.* New Haven: Yale University Press, 1942.

Watson, J. B. *Psychology from the Standpoint of a Behaviorist.* Philadelphia: J. B. Lippincott Company, 1919.

————. *Psychological Care of Infant and Child.* New York: W. W. Norton & Company, Inc., 1928.

White, L. "Energy and Evolution of Culture." *American Anthropology,* 45:335-356 (1943).

Whiting, J. *Becoming a Kwoma.* New Haven: Yale University Press, 1941.

Wissler, C. *Introduction to Social Anthropology.* New York: H. Holt & Company, 1929.

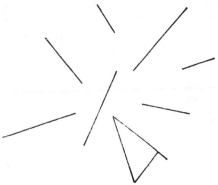

Symbolization and Value

IN WESTERN THOUGHT, A SYMBOL IS
usually something which "represents," which "fits." We "apply" such symbols, as for example, when we "apply" words to things or names to persons; and these symbols then "stand for" the things to which they have been "applied." We even speak of "inventing" symbols; and our social scientists, worried over this age which has lost its values, speak of the need to "create" new symbols, so as to impart value to a meaningless life. This conception of the symbol as something distinct from and applicable to, can be held because of a mode of thinking according to which it is possible and desirable to abstract elements from a total situation, and to separate idea or form from substance. This conception is not a common one outside the province of Western civilization; and in many other cultures, it is inconceivable to make such a split. Here the symbol—the personal name, the picture, the emblem, the word—is an inextricable component of that which to Western thinking, it represents. And indeed there is a widely held theory to the effect that this conception is due to an inability to abstract, that it is the mark of a low stage in the development of the mind, apparently resting in the assumption that when human beings are able to

From *Symbols and Values, an Initial Study*, Thirteenth Symposium of the Conference on Science, Philosophy and Religion, 1954.

abstract, they do so. Yet the most recent scientific thought, the most highly "developed," rejects abstraction as impossible. According to the field theory, elements are considered as incapable of retaining their identity once removed from the field.

The thesis of this essay is that the symbol is in fact a part of a whole, a component of a field which also contains the so-called *thing*, as well as the process of symbolizing, and the apprehending individual. In this view, the concept of the symbol is close to the original meaning of the word in Greek. The *symbol*, the broken off part of the coin given to the parting friend, is not a separate element, but carries with it wherever it goes the whole coin in which it has participated, as well as the situation of hospitality during which the coin was broken in half; and when it is finally matched with the remaining half, the whole has value because the symbol has conveyed—not created or applied or evoked—this value. According to the view presented here, symbols are a part of the process whereby the experienced world, the world of perception and concept, is created out of the world of physical reality, the so-called given, the undifferentiated mass, or energy or set of relations.

The system of symbolization, by means of which the individual punctuates, categorizes, shapes this physical reality, transforming it into the world of sensory perception and concept, is implicit in a variety of behavioral patterns within a culture. Language may be called such a system of symbols or acts of symbolization. It is not a system of names for passively sensed objects and relations already existing in the outer world; but neither does it fit experience into predetermined molds. It is a creative process, in which the individual has an agentive functon; it is part of a field, which contains, in addition, the world of physical reality, the sensing and thinking individual, and the experienced reality. In this way, each word, each grammatical formation, is not an empty label to be applied; it has meaning, not because meaning has been arbitrarily assigned to it, but because it contains the meaning of the concrete situations in which it participates and has participated, and which it has helped create. With participation in situations the meaning of the symbol increases; and when the situation contains value, the symbol itself contains and conveys value. We have societies which proceed on this assumption, and systematically increase the value content of their symbols.

A discussion of language as a system through which the individual transforms physical reality into experienced reality will clarify what I mean. By language, I do not mean only oral or written expression, but the entire system of codification underlying all verbal expression.

According to the classical view, the word is not the *thing*. This object that I hold in my hand is independent of the label I give it. It *is* not a pencil; I only assign to it the name pencil. What *it is*, is assumed to be independent of what *I call it*. Pencil is only a sound-complex, a word for the reality, the *thing*. But the sound aspect of "pencil" is only one aspect of it. When I call this "pencil," I also classify it, as a substantive, a noun; I separate it as other than the fingers it elongates. Is it a *thing* before I call it a pencil?

If it is not, then I am not "applying" a name to an already existing thing. This physical reality, this formless mass or energy, or set of relations, is delimited, is given form and substance, becomes the *thing* pencil, only through my calling it a pencil. In naming it, I give it recognition and a status in the categories of experienced reality. Calling it a pencil is the symbolic process through which I have created it; so that its name, or rather its naming, is a necessary part of itself, without which it is not this *thing*. And, conversely, its name cannot be separated from it as a self-contained element, it has no independent existence as symbol to be applied to an already existing *thing*. A Maidu Indian, for example, would probably have given no recognition to, or would not have delimited this reality into, the pencil as object; instead, he would have perceived the specific act of the hand—in this case the act of pointing with a pencil—and would have expressed this by means of a suffix which, attached to the verb, "to point," means: to-point-with-a-long-thin-instrument (such as a pencil or a straight pipe, or a cigarette, or a stick). There is no reference to substance or to an object in this suffix. What is a pencil to me is a qualification or an attribute of an act for him, and belongs to a class with cigarettes and other objects of this shape only in so far as they elongate the hand making such an act possible. If this can be called a *thing*, then the symbolic process has at any rate helped create different *things* out of the physical reality.

I would say, therefore, that the classical *this* is not the *thing*, but the reality itself. At the point where it is a *thing*, it has already been made into a thing. The word and the thing are not discrete elements to be related by the speaker; they are interdependent, incapable of existence apart from and without the act of the individual.

Again, when we teach our children the proper use of singular and plural, we assume that we are teaching them the proper verbal symbols for already existing singularity and plurality. But in this respect also, we find a difference in other cultures. There is evidence that the Wintu Indians recognize or perceive first of all humanity, human-being-ness, and only secondarily the delimited person. They make no distinction between singular and plural, and a cardinal number is never used with this generic, primary form of the word. They individuate, however, making a particular out of the original generic form of the word; out of *nop*—deermeat or venison—they derive *nopum*—(a) deer; out of *se*—handness, hand—they derive *semum*—finger. Yet here also, unless the Wintu chooses to use a separate word meaning one or several or giving the definite number, there is nothing to show whether the word refers to singular or plural; *nopum* may be one or many individual deer; *semum* may be one or several fingers. When the Wintu want to show that two or more individuals are involved in the same situation, they do not use the *and* to express connection. They will say, "Mary we gathered wood," not: "Mary and I . . ."; "Coyote they mutually-grandmothered dwelled," not: "Coyote and his grandmother dwelled." *We* and *they* are primary; the specific, the singular, is derivative, and seems to be used only by way of clarification. That this is the way they perceive, the *thing* they create, is suggested by the fact that when they are referring to individuals who do not participate in the same situation already, that is, when they bring two individuals together in their statement, they do use the *and*; for example, "Shell *and* Fly (unrelated and living in different villages) each had a son." I find no instance, however, when the *and* is used to connect relatives, or individuals who are intimately connected, to put it in our terms.

The Wintu share this characteristic with many other cultures. Raymond Firth reporting on the Tikopia of the South Pacific, has to explain certain occurrences and terms of speech which are totally unacceptable to Western minds. There was one such occasion during a ceremonial cycle, when he saw several women assembled in a house. He asked a friend what the women were doing there, and received the answer: "The Atua Fafine (the chief Goddess) it is she." For all his efforts, it is impossible for him to make this sound logical and acceptable to people who know that ten women are plural; to people who learn from early childhood that the singular comes first, before the plural; who, when they decline and conjugate start from one and go on to many, who soon learn that one plus one equals two, and later learn to speak of the one and the many, implying the distinction and the hierarchy even when they are questioning it.

When we try to translate terms such as brother and sister into non-Indo-European languages, we become aware of the share which our linguistic categories have in creating the *thing*, the so-called referent of the word. Take the word for brother, for example. In English, its referent is a "male considered in his relation to another having the same parents." Is the in-

dividual to whom I apply this word the *thing*? If the word, "brother,"
merely "stands for" an already existing *thing*, then I should be able to
translate this word successfully into other languages. Only the sound complex will vary; the referent will remain the same.

But when I try to translate this word into Wintu, I find that, in the perceived world of these people there is no such *thing*. I need three words for
his one referent, and one of these words has in addition reference to
something which I recognize as a different *thing*. I need to say *labei*—
"Male considered in relation to a younger male having the same parents,"
or *leikut*—"male considered in relation to an older male . . ."; or I must
say *soh*—"male or female considered in relation to an individual of opposite sex having the same parents." If my word, "brother," refers to a
given, a thing existing irrespective of me and my naming, then the Wintu
and the Turks and the Andamanese and a large number of other societies
perceive falsely; but how can I prove that I am right and all these others
are wrong?

There is further the question of relations; are these found in nature
and does the relational word then merely refer to an already existing relation? According to Western thought, these objects are *on* the table; the
word, "on," refers to the present relationship between objects and table.
Yet a Wintu who saw this might very well say, "The table lumps severally."
At any rate, he does say, "The hill lumps," when I would have said,
"There is a house on the hill," or "a rock on the hill"; and he says, "The
hill lumps-severally," when I would have said, "People have spread their
blankets over the bushes to sun them." In the face of this it is difficult to
maintain that the *thing*, the perceived, is the same in the two cases. In
one case, through the process of symbolization, two disparate objects and
a relation are created; in another, a continuity.

I do not mean to imply by all this that communication is impossible.
Ethnographers in the field have found it possible and even easy to explain
what they mean by the word, "brother," and to understand what their informants meant by their terms for individuals having the same parents.
What this implies, however, is that, for true communication, we cannot
assume as a matter of course that our classifications are the same for people of all cultures; that translation is merely the substitution of one sound-
complex for another. Once we are aware that the basis of classification
is not a universal one, we can find out whether our different words do
name the same thing, and if they do not, we can qualify our word. With
such qualification, the English term can be understood; but I doubt
whether, without repeated usage in relevant situations, this word will con-

vey immediately, for the new user, the same *thing* which it does for the English-speaking ethnographer.

Before I continue with the discussion of the symbol, it should be clear that, to my mind, nothing of what I have said applies to the metaphor, in the literal sense of the word.

Only when the symbol is defined as something made to stand for something else can the two be thought of as similar. There is further the strong possibility that, whereas symbolization is a universal process, the existence of metaphors is limited to those cultures where the definition of the self is that of something discrete and other to everything else. In cultures where the self is not conceived of as entirely disparate from the other, the word which seems to us to be a metaphor is probably only a means of pointing out the participation of one thing in another.

I have tried to establish that the symbol is not a thing, but that it is rather a point in a creative process, that of symbolization, whereby the physical reality is transformed into the *thing*, the experienced reality; that the symbol conveys the meaning of the situation in which it participates, and has no existence and no meaning apart from this situation. When we study societies other than our own, we find that the cultural behavior can often be understood only on the assumption that here, in fact, symbols are regarded as being, rather than standing for, the *thing*. For example, according to Wilson, the priest in ancient Egypt, the symbol of the God, actually *was* God; so that when he was honored or insulted, the God was affected directly through the symbol, not indirectly through a representative. Wilson calls this principle of the participation of the symbol in the *thing*, the principle of consubstantiation. Because of this principle, he holds, it was possible to put small models of loaves of bread into a tomb and know that the dead was eating actual bread. Among primitive societies, we have the Trobrianders, among whom the garden magician performs a magical act in the village garden before every secular agricultural act on the part of the rest of the village group. He works on one standard plot, and only in one corner of this; yet, when he rubs the small corner with his handful of weeds, talking to it persuasively, he is treating the entire village garden. All the garden land has been persuaded to produce good yams.

The Tiv of Nigeria furnish a case where a large group of people perceived the *thing* in its symbol. The case is related by Akiga, a Tiv with a Western education, who was skeptical of the reports of magical killings of which he had heard. At one time he heard that his father had killed and flayed one of his (Akiga's) many sisters, and given her skin to her brother to wear on the occasion of a special ceremonial dance. Akiga went to the dance to see what would happen, and there he saw his brother dancing, holding a woman's filter and his father's pipe. The following day, the people who had gone to the dance were full of the story of how Hilehaan had danced in his sister's skin. They were not trying to deceive anyone; they were talking among themselves, discussing the important event they had witnessed. They had obviously perceived the-skin-of-Hilehaan's-sister (in the filter) who-had-been-flayed-by-her-father (in the father's pipe). Only the Western minded Akiga saw just a filter and a pipe.

In Western civilization, the difference in the conception of the symbol as representing or as participating, constitutes one of the main differences of doctrine between the Catholic Church and most of the Protestant sects. The question at issue is whether, at communion, the bread *represents* the flesh of Christ, or *is* the flesh of Christ.

When "primitives" are said to be incapable of distinguishing the word from the *thing,* or to confuse an object with its name, I suspect that what we have is rather the recognition of this participation of the symbol in the *thing.* When we reflect on our own use of words, we find that with us also, words do more than designate; they have more or less meaning, according to the situations in our personal lives in which they have participated. For example, when I teach, I can use terms for the function of evacuation and for sexual activity freely, so long as I confine myself to Latin words. Otherwise there is discomfort and emotional tension. This does not mean that the Latin terms do not carry the situation in which they have participated. They do; but what they convey is the passage in the textbook, or the paragraph in a dictionary; and these are eminently appropriate to the classroom. When I use the word, "micturition," it carries with it, perhaps, a number of defining words, but not the concrete act. Anglo-Saxon terms for sexual activity would heighten the emotional atmosphere and be very disturbing in the classroom. But not so the Latin terms; they may have participated in love-making in the experience of the Romans, but nobody makes love in Latin nowadays.

This is true also of the words for death or dying. Those of us who have experienced death tend to avoid the symbolizing word in speaking of these situations, because the word conveys the unbearable situation. The need for a term is filled then by a number of substitute terms, such as "passed away" or by differently phrased sentences which avoid the charged word. Yet none of us feels the urge to do this when speaking of people we have not loved. Julius Caesar died; he did not pass away.

The symbol thus gets its meaning through participation in the concrete situation; and it grows in meaning, and even changes in meaning, with each participation. Before it functions in individual experience, it holds no meaning. To the child who hears a word for the first time, the word contains the meaning of the situation in which he hears it, including the mother's tone of voice, her gestures and facial expression. To someone learning the use of a word from a dictionary or from a classroom definition, the word holds only whatever value is present in this situation; probably none. But once the individual uses the newly learned word, once a concrete situation is experienced through the agency of the word, the word contains the value of this symbolized situation. So the symbol, in this case the word, is a thing in process, containing and conveying the value which has become embodied in it, and communicating it in so far as there is community of experience between speaker and hearer.

When I choose a name for my child, for example, I may only choose it because it sounds well with the surname. Perhaps the first time I use the name, I am actually only "applying" it to my newborn daughter. But from this time on, the name is not just a set of syllables, an empty designation. From now on it contains Anna-ness; it is a name not to be taken in vain. This is an attitude which we have officially about the name of God. Yet we do take God's name in vain, and in situations where we would not welcome his presence, apparently firm in our belief that the name does not convey the *thing*.

Those of us who are concerned with the meaningless life of our industrial society speak of the need for introducing value through creating new symbols. But symbols in themselves have no value, and they cannot convey value to a situation. Only after they have participated in a situation can they have value, and then only in so far as the situation itself holds value.

In conclusion, I shall speak about the Bella Coola of British Columbia whose culture was based upon the definition of the symbol as I have presented it here, and who proceed deliberately and carefully to incorporate value in their symbols through having them participate in situations which they imbued with value for this purpose.

Among the Bella Coola, an individual was not complete without a name. He had no definition, no validity, no status without a name. He could not become a chief, or a hunter, or a carpenter without the necessary symbolic ingredient. The names were embodied in family myths, and carried with them certain prerogatives with which they become imbued at the special mythical occurrence during which they originated. Names did not "stand for." When they had become duly validated, when they belonged to a person as the symbolic component, they could be loaned over a period of time, or rented out, or given away as a gift; and the name was no more part of the man to whom it had belonged up until that time. At death, a man's names died with him. They were now in the burial ground, empty of value.

An infant lacked value as well as validity and social place at birth. If he was the child of a slave, he had minus value, unless this had been "washed away" in the womb through a special ceremonial gift-giving. When a child was born, a family name was resurrected to be given to the newborn. But the name at this time was "as nothing." It was weak; and the prerogatives it contained could not be validly assumed. It was necessary to give validity to the act of giving the name, and to infuse value into the name.

For the Bella Coola, the process of validation of this introduction of the symbolic component consisted of displaying the whole situation—the name with the embodied prerogatives and the myth from which they derived—in a structured public situation; and in this display, in the singing of the song which the prerogative contains, in the recounting of that portion of the myth in which it is embedded, the symbol participated in the situation. But, for the symbol to acquire value, the situation must have value; and the Bella Coola proceeded to imbue the situation with value.

The creation of value consisted of giving a gift; and the value created was exactly equal to the value of the gift. When a name was given to a child, or assumed by an adult, and thereafter whenever any of its ingredients were publicly displayed, gifts were given away. As the gift was given, it was "emptied" of value; it became "nothing." Its value flowed "away" into the name which was being publicly displayed. The gifts made the name "bright," "strong," "heavy," "firm," "clear," "upright"; and the strengthening of the name was the strengthening of the individual, so no clear distinction was made between the two. Occasions for strengthening a name or for assuming a new name, and particularly of those which carried with them the prerogative of a special seat, required the accumulation of large amounts of property, and often included a number of specific ceremonials—such as the dance of the returned dead—and necessitate the invitation of widely scattered guests, so that the display might be sufficiently public.

Eventually, as the occasions increased in extent, as a man's wife "drags across" enough names—prerogatives properly validated—and as enough other gifts had been given away to "shield him from the fire," to "make him strong and heavy as he moves about the earth," to "make his seat soft," to "shore him up so he does not wobble," the occasions became extensive enough to be potlatches. After giving four potlatches, a man has accumulated enough value inside himself to be considered a chief; now "he is so strong, he can go where he will." In all this, it is never clear whether reference is made to the symbolic component or to the whole individual, "the thing." [1]

The exercise of a craft or a profession was the display of a prerogative and must always be validated; and with each such display, the value of the prerogative was increased. A man could have the physical skill of hunting, the knowledge and judgment necessary, but he could not be effective, he could not be a hunter without the duly validated symbolic component. On the other hand, as the prerogative was strengthened through repeated display, it might become eventually stronger than the rest of the man, than, for example, his (material) knowledge. This was particularly the case of the profession of warrior. Those who had the prerogative of being warriors, had to kill upon request—without fee, since this was the display of the prerogative. McIlwraith tells the story of one such warrior, who was sick of killing, yet could not stop, as his prerogative had become too strong for him through his repeated killings. In the end, he retired into a cave one winter, and his dead body was found there the following spring; this was the only way he could stop killing.

A precisely formulated case of creating value was found in the so-called coppers of the Bella Coola. These were thin pieces of copper of a special shape and size, which were displayed at public occasions, and eventually were destroyed to "make bone" for a returned dead relative. A copper, whose recognized value was known as three hundred dollars was broken in two, or thrown into the fire; its value flowed out of it and into the dead. Now the copper, which a minute ago was full of value, became completely empty of value.

Presently the owner of the copper picked it up and gave it to a poor man, who cleaned and straightened and repaired it and sold it to a chief for perhaps twenty dollars which could be spent only for acquiring food to be given away publicly. That is, the twenty dollars were given away as a gift to infuse value into the copper, which now contained value to the

---

[1] It should be made clear here that, for value to be accumulated in the name, no return gifts must be given. To do so would be a deliberate act of destruction. However, other gifts were in fact also given by the individual, increasing his prestige, his non-symbolic aspect. Such gifts did not "become nothing." The giving of such a gift diminished the recipient by as much as it increased the giver. If the gift was not returned, the recipient remained diminished in being; if an equal gift was returned, he recovered only his original stature. It was to his interest then, not only to return the gift, but to exceed the received gift as much as he could, even to double it. When he did so, the original giver became diminished, and proceeded to give a larger gift, as soon as he could do so. These were not validating gifts, and did not have to form a part of the potlatch, though they usually did so; and they were clearly distinguished from those gifts whose value "flows away" into the symbol.

degree of twenty dollars. The chief now proceeded to increase the value of the copper. Perhaps he gave it a name with the appropriate public display; and he gave away fifty dollars to validate the display. He next invited guests, displayed the copper, had it passed from hand to hand—had it fully participate in the event—and gave away gifts to the amount of eighty dollars. He did this gradually, for all growth was a matter of time. He could not merely assign a value to it; nor could he infuse value into it all at once. Eventually, when enough value had been imbued, so that the copper could function at a dance of the returned dead, the owner flung it in the fire, and again it was emptied of its value.

The white traders quickly spotted the importance of the coppers, and before long had flooded the market with them. They thought of them naturally as having value, or as representing value; perhaps as analogous to our paper money. But the coppers neither had nor lacked value in themselves. They were symbols only in the sense in which the symbol has been presented here; they acquired and conveyed only the value inherent in the situation in which they participated. No one wanted to buy a copper unless he was ready to go through the long and expensive procedure of infusing it with value. So the flood of coppers brought no inflation; the value of coppers neither could rise nor fall, through such manipulation. Being true symbols, they could acquire valid existence and value only through participation in meaningful situations.

REFERENCES

Akiga's Story, the Tiv Tribe as seen by one of its Members, translated and annotated by Rupert East. London: Oxford University Press, 1939.

Dixon, Roland B. "Maidu." *Handbook of American Indian Languages*, edited by Franz Boas, Bulletin 40, Part I, Washington, 1911.

Firth, Raymond. *The Work of the Gods in Tikopia*. London: Lund, Humphries & Co., Ltd., 1940.

Lee, Dorothy. "Linguistic Reflection of Wintu Thought." *International Journal of American Linguistics*, 10:181-187 (1944).

————. "Notes on the Conception of the Self Among the Wintu Indians.' *Journal of Abnormal and Social Psychology*, 45:538-543 (1950).

————. "Being and Value in a Primitive Culture." *Journal of Philosophy*, 46:401-415 (1949).

McIlwraith, T. F. *The Bella Coola Indians*. Toronto: University of Toronto Press 1948.

Malinowski, Bronislaw. *Coral Gardens and Their Magic*. New York: American Book Company, 1935.

Wilson, John A. "Egypt." In Frankfort, Henri and Henrietta A. *The Intellectual Adventure of Ancient Man*. Chicago: University of Chicago Press, 1946.

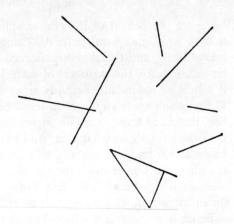

Being and Value in
a Primitive Culture

THE TROBRIANDERS[1] ARE CONCERNED
with being, and being alone. Change and becoming are foreign to their
thinking. An object or event is grasped and evaluated in terms of itself
alone, that is, irrespective of other beings. The Trobriander can describe

[1] These people have been studied intensively by Professor Bronislaw Malinowski, who
has published his results in several monographs. This essay is based on his writings and
refers to the Trobrianders as they were when Malinowski knew them. If at times I
venture to disagree with Professor Malinowski's own deductions, it is only because, in
presenting the material with such a wealth of pertinent detail and emotional association,
he has made it possible for his readers to draw their own conclusions.

The Trobriand Islands lie to the east of New Guinea. They are in water where
marine life abounds. The bush is full of plants producing edible fruit. When Malinowski
lived there, the population was sparse enough so that hunger became a menace only
in the rare years of drought. Yet here we find a society of people who work hard,
though nature does not compel them to do so. The men rise early in the morning, to
go to the fields, of their own will, so as to cultivate yams which they will not consume;
or to go to work at overhauling or building canoes which shall serve to take them on
dangerous voyages to bring back ornaments which cannot be used for their own
adornment, and which can be possessed for only a few months. The men are honest
in their dealings, they observe the taboos and fulfill their many obligations though
there is no direct political or social control over their activities.

From *Journal of Philosophy*, No. 13, June 23, 1949, Vol. 46.

being for the benefit of the ethnographer; otherwise, he usually refers to it by a word, one word only. All being, to be significant, must be Trobriand being, and therefore experienced at the appropriate time as a matter of course by the members of each Trobriand community; to describe it would be redundant. Being is never defined, in our sense of the word. Definition presents an object in terms of *what it is like* and *what it is unlike*, that is, in terms of its distinguishing characteristics. The Trobriander is interested only in *what it is*. And each event or being is grasped timelessly; in our terms, it contains its past, present, and future, but these distinctions are non-existent for the Trobriander. There is, however, one sense in which being is not self-contained. To be, it must be part of an ordained pattern; this aspect will be elaborated below.

Being is discrete and self-contained; it has no attributes outside of itself. Its qualities are identical with it and without them it is not itself. It has no predicate; it is itself. To say a word representing an object or act is to imply the existence of this, and all the qualities it incorporates. If I were to go with a Trobriander to a garden where the taytu, a species of yam, had just been harvested, I would come back and tell you: "There are good taytu there; just the right degree of ripeness, large and perfectly shaped; not a blight to be seen, not one rotten spot; nicely rounded at the tips, with no spiky points; all first-run harvesting, no second gleanings." The Trobriander would come back and say "Taytu"; and he would have said all that I did and more.

Even the phrase "There are taytu" would represent a tautology, since existence is implied in being, is, in fact an ingredient of being to the Trobriander. And all the attributes, even if he could find words for them at hand in his own language, would have been tautological, since the concept of taytu contains them all. In fact, if one of these were absent, the object would not have been a taytu. Such a tuber, if it is not at the proper harvesting ripeness, is not a taytu. If it is unripe, it is a bwanawa; if overripe, spent, it is not a spent taytu but something else, a yowana. If it is blighted it is a nuunokuna. If it has a rotten patch, it is a taboula; if misshapen, it is an usasu; if perfect in shape but small, it is a yogogu. If the tuber, whatever its shape or condition, is a post-harvest gleaning, it is an ulumadala. When the spent tuber, the yowana, sends its shoots underground, as we would put it, it is not a yowana with shoots, but a silisata. When new tubers have formed on these shoots, it is not a silisata but a gadena. An object can not change an attribute and retain its identity. Some range of growth or modification within being is probably allowed, otherwise speech would be impossible; but I doubt whether they are conscious of it. As soon as such change, if we may introduce one of our concepts here, is officially recognized, the object ceases to be itself.

As being is identical with the object, there is no word for *to be*; as being is changeless, there is no word meaning *to become*. Becoming involves temporality, but Trobriand being has no reference to time. With us, change in time is a value, and place in a developmental sequence is necessary for evaluation. We can not respond with approval or disapproval, unless we know that a thing is getting bigger or better or surer. If I am told that Robert Smith is an instructor at $3000, I cannot respond to this adequately, unless I know that he is just out of graduate school, or that he used to be a professor at the age of forty, but now, at sixty, he has been demoted to this position.

Our language is full of terms such as the one I have just used—demotion—giving us tools for the evaluation of being in terms of place in a climactic historical sequence. By dint of constant vigilance, we can refrain from using these terms; but we have no choice when it comes to placing events in time. Our language codifies reality in such a way as to predispose us to view events in terms of temporality. Even if I decide to use such expressions as "it be" or "it flow," I have achieved nothing, since you who hear me automatically make these acceptable to yourself by translating them into "it is" and "it flows," merely putting me down as uneducated.

Whenever I make an assertion, I have to give it temporal limits, in reference to past, present, or future, or at any rate I have to imply temporality. Trobriand verbs are timeless, making no temporal distinctions. A Trobriander can, if he chooses, refer to an act as completed, but that, it seems to me, is an aspect of the act, not a temporal reference. History and mythical reality are not "the past" to the Trobriander. They are forever present, participating in all current being, giving meaning to all his activities and all existence. A Trobriander will speak of the garden which his mother's brother planted, or the one which the mythical Tudava planted, in exactly the same terms with which he will refer to the garden which he himself is planting now; and it will give him satisfaction to do so.

Being is apprehended as a whole, not in terms of attributes. This is something very difficult for members of our culture to achieve; we rarely value sheer being in itself, except perhaps when we are "blindly" in love. Even mothers are often incapable of valuing their children in this way, demanding instead attributes and achievements before they will respond with love. I watched one of my students once in a predicament created by this inability to react to being itself. Faced with a vivid, gurgling infant in the presence of its mother, she felt it necessary to react but had no basis for doing so. She tried hard to discover attributes to guide her, asking, "Does she talk?" "Does she creep?" hoping for something on which to base approval; and, finally, having received a negative answer to all her questions, she remained dumb and immobilized. The Trobriander does not say, "how bright" or "how big"; his equivalent in this situation would have been "how baby."

Being is evaluated discretely, in terms of itself alone, not in comparison with others. This, again, is foreign to our thinking, except perhaps in the sphere of art. To return to Robert Smith, if you tell me that he is an instructor at $3000 a year, I can respond to this with approbation, commiseration, etc., only if I know what the pay of other men instructors is apt to be. To evaluate, I have to compare this being with other beings of its kind. To be good, being has to be as good as, if not better than. For the Trobriander, being is good only as itself.

Now our own language makes it easy, though not imperative, to compare beings at every turn. It provides us with a large number of comparatives, through morphology and vocabulary. Our speech is studded with terms such as better, bigger, inferior, average, compared to, normal, equal, in relation to, etc., showing that we constantly are passing judgment according to a comparative standard. The Trobriander has no such means, unless we accept his rarely used words "it-sames" and "it-differents" as comparative. The magic formulas given by Malinowski are full of similes, as only in this way can they be made comprehensible to his readers. But in Trobriand, these are all metaphors. Where Malinowski's translation reads, for example, "thy shoots are as quick as the eyes of the black ant," the Trobriand text reads, "no thine eye, thine eye black-ant." When Malinowski says, "I am your senior," the Trobriand text reads, "old man I."

We can see this emphasis on *being* alone when we analyze the Trobriand sentence. Here we find that the words are presented discretely, without elements to show the relation of one word to the other. A verb contains its subject, a noun contains its "predicate" as well as its other attributes. The few words which Malinowski translated as adjectives are either nouns—a big-one, or verbs—it-goods. The language does not even express an object-to-object relationship, as ours does, for example, when it relates grammatical subject to the object which is acted upon. In English, we express this relationship through word order; when we say, for example, "Mary ate the pie," or, "John kicked Mary," [2] we clearly distinguish the actor from the one acted upon, by order of precedence, and we can not avoid making the distinction. The Trobriander, on the other hand, merely expresses act and participants; "i-wo-ye tau" "it-beat-man" means either that the man is beating someone or that someone is beating the man. Such a phrase usually refers either to a known situation, which needs no elucidation, or is told within a context which makes its meaning clear. If, however, the Trobriander for some reason feels that he must specify, he can do so; but he does not do so as a matter of course, as we do, since his language does not predispose or constrain him to do so.

To be, an object must be true to itself, not in terms of its relationship with other beings. To be good, it must be the same always. Sameness is a value to the Trobrianders. Trobriand being never came into existence; it has always been, exactly as now, above ground in "historic" [3] times, below ground in mythical times. At some time the ancestress of each group emerged from a specific hole, bringing with her all the customs, skills, and beliefs of that group, their patterns of behavior, the details of their magic, their pedigreed yams. This "past" is immanent in all Trobriand being. Instead of description in terms of attributes, the Trobriander gives an account of historical or mythical past, presenting essence. In all his undertakings, this "past" is present, giving to them validity and value. Wherever he goes, his surroundings have meaning for him; every waterhole, rock, or cleft is imbued with mythical significance.

Myth and history, as intrinsic to being, enhance value. For example, the Trobrianders have certain important valuables which constitute the gifts in the *kula*, an endless circular series of ceremonial gift-givings which occupies, with the preparation involved, perhaps half the life of Trobriand men. These objects have value, but no "utility"; they are "ornaments" which can not be used to adorn the "owner"; and they can be possessed only a few months by each recipient. Giving-in-itself, that is, non-purposive giving, is good; through participation in this gift-giving pattern the kula

[2] That it is word order, not the rarely present morphology, on which we depend, is evident from the fact that when we hear, "John kicked she," we automatically change this to "John kicked her." We correct the morphology, understanding the statement according to order. If we depended on morphology for the expression of relationship, we would have understood it according to the morphology, and corrected the statement into, "She kicked John." In American English at present, we use morphological distinction in this connection for purposes of esthetics, or even snobbery, not for clarity.

[3] I use quotation marks for terms which we, from the point of view of our own culture, would apply; terms which would otherwise require cumbersome qualification whenever they appear.

valuables are good. Each valuable is named and its personal history known. In this lies much of its value; giver and recipient, and even the village of the "owner," get satisfaction out of the recounting of the specific kula acts of which the article was a part, going from named giver to named recipient. Chronology and historical sequence are irrelevant; the history is important not as development but as the ingredient of being.

The Trobriander has no word for history. When he wants to distinguish between different kinds of occasions, he will say, for example, "Molubabeba in-child-his," that is, "in the childhood of Molubabeba," not a previous phase of *this* time, but a different kind of time. For him, history is an unordered repository of anecdote; he is not interested in chronological sequence. For example, Malinowski recorded an account of a famine which was given with complete disregard to chronology; an effect which is achieved only deliberately by our sophisticated writers. If we rearrange the clusters of statements so that they represent for us a historical sequence, we have to give them in the following order: one, four, three, two, five.

For us, chronological sequence is of vital importance, largely because we are interested not so much in the event itself, but rather in its place within a *related* series of events; we look for its antecedents and its consequences. We are concerned with the causal or telic relationship between events or acts. To the Trobriander, events do not fall of themselves into a pattern of causal relationships, as they do for us. I am not here concerned with the question of whether causality is given, or is read into existence. Whichever may be the case, we in our culture automatically see and seek relationships, not being itself, and express relationship mainly in terms of cause or purpose. The maddeningly persistent question of our young children is "why," because this is the question implicit in most of our ordinary statements and other behavior, and we answer either in causal or telic terms, since cause and purpose are equally dynamic for us, and are identified in the reference of "why."

Esthetically, as well as practically, cause and purpose are both important to us; cause gives us a satisfying explanation and purpose ennobles or gives meaning to the act. We teach the importance of purposive action to infants, directly and indirectly by act and speech. We teach it in the schoolroom, in sports, in politics, in moral precept. The unreflective scientist takes causation for granted, the orthodox historian studies history to discover the causes for events. To the Trobriander, on the other hand, being or event remains discrete, sufficient unto itself, true and of value as itself, judged and motivated and understood in terms of itself alone. In the face of this apprehension of being, concepts such as causation and purpose appear irrelevant; I have introduced them here only because they are so basic to our thinking that we accept them as given in experience, and their presence is assumed by us in all cultures, as a matter of course.[4]

In the language of the Trobrianders, there are no terms such as because, so as to, cause, reason, effect, purpose, to this end, so that, why. This does not mean that the Trobrianders are incapable of explaining a sequence in terms of cause and effect, but rather that this relationship is of no significance. In the texts given by Malinowski *for* (pela) occurs occasionally, in such a context that it is possible to translate it as *because*, as Malinowski does, and it sounds natural that one should do so; and, once or twice, what-thing-for is used in such a position that we can take it to mean *for what purpose*. It is significant that "pela" is verbal, meaning *to jump*, not a connecting link but a leap to an other. I shall not go here into a discussion of the meaning of the doubtful "pela"; I do not think it is an expression of causality, but even if it is, it occurs extremely rarely and does not contradict the conclusion that, for the Trobriander, events do not automatically fall into the mold of causality of teleology. Malinowski's frequent "why" evoked from the Trobrianders either confused and self-contradictory answers, or the usual "It was ordained of old,"—not an explanation but a description of value, tautological but necessary for the questioning ethnographer.

We ask here, how is influence or motivation or effect phrased among the Trobrianders? How is magical action understood, for example? The answer is, it is understood in exactly these terms, as action, not cause. The magician does not *cause* certain things to be; he *does* them. As the gardener with his material implements burns the brush, breaks the clods, etc., so the garden magician with his various formulas "awakens the sprout," "drives up the shoots overground," "throws the headgear of the taytu," "makes several branches," "pushes the taytu tubers into the soil," according to Trobriand account. This is not influence, nor the force of magic; rather it is "to magic."

Malinowski, in presenting accounts of magic, uses purposive phraseology, since in this way only can his readers understand magic. But where he gives in translation: The okwala rite is made so that taytu might really

---

[4] This absence of causal concepts, as well as of a comparative standard, seemed at first so striking to me that I wrote a paper describing Trobriand thought in terms of what it was not, as non-causal and non-comparative. It now seems to me that I was viewing the Trobrianders then through the eyes of my own culture, relationally, seeing them according to what they were unlike, and so stressing the absence of concepts which have no relevance to their thought.

grow, so that it might ripen, the Trobriander has actually said: okwala, it-grow truly, it-ripen; just a number of events. It so happens, in the example, that the sequence in the account corresponds to the actual order of fact; but quite often there is not even such correspondence. And in the acts themselves there is often not even the sequence into which we could at least read causality. For example, when the Trobriander wants to fell a tree he first exorcizes the tokway, the tree-dwelling spirit, reciting a spell which gets the tokway down. After that he gives the tokway some food. If the food was offered first, on the ground, or at least promised, we could see this as a causal inducement. Actually, the tokway has no alternative and no freedom of choice at all; he is brought down by the spell. The offering of the food itself is merely part of the established procedure, and is not causally related to the exorcism.

It follows that the Trobriander performs acts because of the activity itself, not for its effects; that he values objects because they are good, not good for; in fact, objects and activities that are good for, are of no value to him. Take, for example, his yams and his yam gardening. To Malinowski, who spent many months with them, dependent upon them socially as well as materially, gardening meant yam gardening, and food meant yams. It was only after he had occupied himself with his Trobriander material for about fifteen years and written several books on the subject, that he realized that taro was an ancient and substantial item of food, much easier to grow than yams, less demanding of care and good soil, perhaps almost as important as yams from the point of view of sheer material nourishment. But taro is only good for; it is only good for food, or, less than that, for stopping hunger; and it is grown for such use. Therefore it was of no value or importance to the Trobriander, and escaped Malinowski's notice. Yams, on the other hand, incorporate the social good. They are good in themselves, and participate daily in good situations, as free, nonutile gifts.

A man gardens yams with the expenditure of much care and effort, with physical and magical skills, putting in long, hot hours of work. He gardens as many plots as he is capable of—not as many as his neighbors, or as many as he "needs." About half of these he sets aside as the urigubu plots. These he harvests with pride, exhibiting beautiful heaps of taytu. Then he sends this harvest, by festively arrayed youths and maidens, not to his yam house, but to the hamlet of his sister's husband. In this man's garden the taytu are heaped again, and it is this man now who exhibits them with pride as the gift. Finally, his yam house is put in order, and magic is performed in it. Ideally, the magic makes the taytu rot uneaten in the yam house; it fills the owners with nausea at the thought of eating the taytu; it gives them, instead, an urge to go to the bush and eat what grows there. This keeps the taytu free of purpose; ideally, they are not food.

Taytu are constantly being given and received as gifts, in a system of free giving without what we call ulterior motives; not for altruism, not in barter or exchange for. Most of the gift taytu are usually eaten eventually, but only incidentally. In the urigubu gardens of the man who grew them, have remained all the tubers which are not taytu; the ones which are misshapen, or unduly small or blighted in some way. These go to the gardener's not-good yam house. They are merely to be eaten, and we do not hear of them again. The taytu, however, have a very important place in the everyday, as well as the ceremonial, life of the people. Taytu are not, like the taro, good for. Taytu have value, not use; value lies in being, not in relationship.

The pariahs among the Trobrianders are the people who barter. There is one such unfortunate district of highly skilled manufacturers who have no adequate soil for the growing of taytu. They barter manufactured articles, spending their time in this not-good occupation, but more than that, they are lacking in the growing of taytu and in pure gift-giving, that is, in good. They are greatly despised by the agricultural villages.

The coastal villages also can not grow many yams, and acquire more through what seems to us an exchange of fish for yams. However, this has been patterned along gift-giving lines, and escapes the purposiveness of barter. A man of a specific interior village will have a life-long gift-partner in a fishing village. Whenever he wants to, he arrives at the fishing village with some baskets of yams, and leaves them as a gift at a specific spot. This precipitates a pattern of events which ends in his returning home with a gift of fish. He can not go to *any* village with his taytu, or to *any* man within this village; the gift to anyone else would have no meaning, neither would it induce anyone else to go fishing. His taytu were not pay or inducement, but the opening step in a specific patterned procedure involving a specific individual.

Here another aspect of Trobriand being is involved. I have spoken of being as discrete, and apprehended as itself alone. I must now qualify this statement. Being has no independent existence. It is itself only as part of an established pattern. To members of our culture, being is defined by its attributes, relationships, and functions; temporally in terms of becoming, spatially in terms of its relationships. For the Trobrianders, being is defined by a fixed place in an established pattern. It is perhaps too much to ask my readers to believe that one element in a pattern can be and is perceived only in terms of its specific position within the pattern itself, and without reference to any other element; that in fact a pattern is conceived as something other than a system of relationships. Nevertheless, I believe such to be the case among the Trobrianders. Being is not seen in terms of its relationships to a plurality of elements in the pattern, but rather as a fixed point in a single, changeless whole. Only in this place can being be itself; only as it fills its place is it desired or valued.

Being is good and true in terms of pattern. Gift-giving, for example, is good only within a patterned Trobriand situation. It is neither virtuous nor altruistic; both these terms involve meaningless relational concepts. In Trobriand gift-giving, the need of the recipient, or the effect upon him, is not involved. I doubt whether the Trobrianders could be persuaded to send yams to the starving Bikinians; and even if they did send yams, their act would not have value. The harvest gift to the sister's husband is not an act of altruism. The giver is concerned only with fulfilling his role, his place in a specific Trobriand pattern. If he gave taro to his sister's husband, the gift would not have been good; if he gave the yams to his own brother, his act would not have been good. What is good in this situation is the *urigubu*. To be good, this gift must be urigubu; to be true, that is, to be urigubu, it must be, (a) a gift of taytu; (b) from man to sister's husband; (c) at harvest time.

Both the good and the true are defined by place in pattern. Taytu figure as gifts upon different occasions, between different individuals. In each case the gift is named and valued differently. When Taytu are given to a friend at the launching of a canoe, they follow a different procedure, and are kabigodoya; when they are a harvest gift to a specialist, they are a kari-budaboda. Taytu, then, are urigubu, kabigodoya, karibudaboda, according to their place in different patterns; and each gift derives different being, and different value in accordance to the pattern in which it has place. I should explain here that in each case the taytu remain taytu though they participate in different situations; it is the gift which is different according to its place in a different pattern.

This conception of being and value gave the early pearl traders much trouble. They found out soon that money or the things they offered were no inducement to work. They noticed, however, that the Trobrianders set great store by certain large blades made of stone. At first, they had these imitated carelessly, but found that the natives did not want them; then they had them made of slate in Europe, but these also were rejected by the Trobrianders. Finally they had the native stone quarried and sent to Parisian craftsmen; but these beautiful blades also were rejected. These things, of course, could not be valued, since they were not truly Trobri- and, had not been made "as ordained of old"; but more than that, they could not be an inducement, and could have no meaning, since they were external to the pattern. When the Trobrianders were finally persuaded to dive for pay, it was only the natives of those villages which had always dived for oysters who were persuaded; those of the other coastal villages, where diving had not been ordained of old, would not dive. And the na- tives of the appropriate villages did so grudgingly. To the disgust of the pearl traders, they would leave their diving and go off fishing for the day, as soon as a number of baskets of yams made their appearance on the beach, even though the traders offered them twenty times as many yams. The natives would work for extraneous inducement as long as there was no good undertaking to indulge in; but when their gift-partners arrived with yams, they initiated a patterned situation which had meaning for the natives.

You will say, "But is not this an inducement or cause?" I think it is not. By themselves, the few baskets of yams on the beach are just a few baskets of yams. Offered by the trader they would have had no meaning. Brought from a different Trobriand village, they would have effected nothing; and when they come from the appropriate village, it is only the partners of the specific givers who go off fishing as a matter of course. Given from anyone to anyone, the taytu are of no value.

The yams are not an inducement to action, to my mind. The giving of them, however, starts a pattern; once the gift has taken place, the pattern becomes evident and the recipient is presented with a role which holds value for him; to get satisfaction from it, to be a good Trobriander, he must fill it. By us, the two acts, the receiving of the yams and the procuring of the fish, are seen in relationship; and this relationship is seen as dynamic; one act influences the other, or causes the other. To the Trobriander, what is dynamic is the validity and value derived from the pattern. The coastal villager goes fishing because (this is my own word) he gets satisfaction from fulfilling his role in the pattern.

The appearance of the baskets of yams is not a cause, but it does pre- cipitate a pattern. The Trobrianders have their own equivalent for cause, in terms of their concept of pattern. For this they use the term "u'ula," a word very commonly used, for what we would call a variety of meanings. It stands for the trunk of a tree below the branches; for the base of a pole, or the bottom of a structure; it means the organizer of an expedition or the initiator of any undertaking; it refers to the first part of a magical formula.

The u'ula is sometimes contemporaneous with the rest of the object or pattern, sometimes not. To the Trobriander, I think, it indicates place, not temporality. Realized or not, the pattern is always there; the pole has a bottom, the spell a beginning; and this pattern is known as a whole, not as a temporal process. Once brought into the actual through the u'ula, the total must be realized. To this extent, and in our terms only, can we understand u'ula to be the equivalent of *cause*; the u'ula is dynamic but only in reference to the pattern, not toward the next event. The u'ula precipitates the next event but only incidentally, because it precipitates the patterned procedure, through its place in the pattern; it so happens that the next event is a part of this pattern.

This is how we can understand the "actual" and mythical behavior of the Trobrianders. For example, when an uvalaku, a kula expedition of a special kind, has been organized to sail to distant tribes where the Trobrianders will receive as gifts certain necklaces from specific partners, the chief gives a kayguya'u, a great ceremonial distribution of food. This is an act very serious in its implications, and performed after much consultation and deliberation; because, once this kayguya'u is given, the expedition must be carried out to its end, however unfavorable the winds, or the conditions within the village. Once the pattern has been initiated, the whole must be realized, or, to put it differently, the whole is inevitably there; I am floundering here because my language can not reproduce the Trobriand identity of the concepts underlying *has been, must be,* and *is.* Knowing the pattern, the Trobriander knows how to act to the end of the pattern. Conversely, the kayguya'u is an u'ula, has meaning, and can even be said to be itself, only by virtue of its place in the uvalaku pattern. Outside of it, it is just another food-distribution, initiating nothing, unless it is something else as part of another pattern.

For us, not only purpose, but previous action, is used as a basis or guide for determining what to do next. For the Trobriander, who does not see acts in relation, pattern is the "guide"; though actually it does not "lead" him to a decision, since his act is predetermined by the pattern. There is a sequence in one of the myths which exemplifies this. Toweyre kills his brother who has been acting in an unTrobriand fashion, working for individual ends. This act of Toweyre is not part of a Trobriand pattern; however, this does not mean that he now has to come to an independent decision on how to act on the basis of murdering his brother. A brother's death itself initiates a pattern. As the next of kin,[5] Toweyre goes back to the village and instructs his dead brother's children to prepare

---

[5] In Trobriand society, a man's children and his father are not his kin.

the body for the funeral, and he himself arranges for the appropriate food distribution, the sagali.

Within the pattern the Trobriander feels safe and acts with assurance. Away from home, he likes to reproduce known previous order, even physically. When a food distribution, a sagali, is given to which many different hamlets from a distance are invited, the geographic location of these hamlets is reproduced on the beach. (I am afraid it is impossible for me to show conclusively that this is not an interest in relative position.) Again, in one of the myths is given a description of a shipwreck, a dreadful event since it plunges the sailors into witch-infested waters. The crew of the large canoe drift ashore clinging to the outrigger, onto which they have jumped from their places in the canoe. As they reach shore, they are in great danger from the flying witches; in the face of it, they walk in exactly the order in which they have drifted ashore; when they sit waiting for night to come and hide them from the witches, they maintain this order; in this order they finally march to their village where they are medicated magically to free them from danger. Now they are safe again, and the order need not be maintained. Again, it is impossible for people of our culture not to see here the order of lineal relationship; but I do not think that it appears as relational to the Trobrianders.

For members of our culture, value lies ideally in change, in moving away from the established pattern; and safety is ensured through scientific prediction, not exact experience. We hopefully expect next year to be better, brighter, different; if, as we hope, it brings change, we can safely meet it with the use of logic and science. Our advertisers thrive on this value of the different, the not-experienced; our industries have long depended on our love for new models. The Trobriander, on the contrary, expects and wants next year to be the same as this year and as the year before his culture emerged from underground. Advertising is nonsense for the Trobriander, because the new is not good and the old is known and valued, so to talk about it persuasively is nonsense. In repetition of the experienced, in sameness, he finds, not boredom, but satisfaction as well as safety. Members of our culture go into uncharted seas fearlessly, depending on compass and the science of navigation; they explore new lands eagerly. The Trobrianders go into *known* waters; they recount the kula myths, and then go from known landmark to known landmark, myth-imbued and full of history; they do not even set their course by the stars or the sun. They repeat old journeyings, their own or those of mythical or historical kula figures.

Something must be said here about individual and pattern; how does an individual Trobriander enter a pattern? There are various ways in which he does so and we in our culture would distinguish them according to the principle of whether he enters automatically, or whether he does so by act of will. By virtue of being born, an individual enters certain patterns of behavior in terms of certain people, those, for example, who are his relatives by blood or affinity. Here he has no choice; the pattern happens to him through the accident of his birth. Again, when his sister marries, or his wife dies, or his kula partner arrives, this precipitates a pattern of activities involving his participation, where he has no choice, unless, of course, he is ready to be unTrobriand. There are certain patterns, however, where he does have freedom of choice: here, whether the pattern is to be precipitated or not, devolves on an act of will of his own. This is the only point where he does have freedom of choice; once he initiates the pattern, he must follow an established procedure.

However, I think the concept of freedom of choice is incommensurate with Trobriand value or behavior, and, in fact, a false measure. For us, to act as we want to act necessarily involves freedom of choice, but for the Trobriander the concept is meaningless. I think the Trobriander has no more and no less freedom when he initiates than when he continues an ordained pattern. In each case, he acts as he wants to, because the act, and the pattern which validates it, holds satisfaction for him; he acts in this way because he is Trobriand, and the pattern is Trobriand. To be Trobriand is to be good. "Act of will" and "freedom of choice" are irrelevant as principles of classification or evaluation.

Then comes the question of whether all beings are part of a pattern, and its corollary: is all being good? Is any being good apart from pattern? I do not think that all being is good; rather, that the good, or value, is found in being, but not in all being. There is much giving going on daily, but it is not good giving; it may be merely desultory giving from husband to wife or a man to his brother—gift situations which are not part of any gift pattern. Much of the unpatterned everyday behavior is not good; eating is not good, nor is love-magic, or love-making. On the other hand, some being is good apart from the pattern in which it participates. Such are the vaygu'a with which the pearl traders failed so miserably; such also is the taytu. In each case the history of these is a pattern in itself.

The taytu, for example, is planted and grown according to an ordained pattern. Each part of the procedure is inaugurated by a garden magician, and no member of the gardening group can act independently, can choose to leave his scrub not burned or have it burned at a different time, or set fire to it himself rather than wait for the magician to do the initial firing.

At one time the resident magistrate ignorantly set fire to the scrub himself and thus initiated a year of drought. On the other hand, taro is not good; but none of the activities concerned with it are patterned. The gardener in this case proceeds as he likes, and incorporates whatever magic he chooses into the process. Ultimately, then, it is pattern that bestows value; but good being may incorporate its own pattern. Whether this is a difference between good being (taytu or kula givings) and not-good being (taro and gifts to one's brother) or whether it is rather a difference between being and mere existence, I am not qualified to say.

Is the Trobriander truly blind to relationship? Does he never respond to external motivation? The gardening of the Trobriander certainly can be seen as work toward the end of growing yams. Obviously—to us—when a man gives the harvest gift, this act brings giver and receiver into relation; how can the Trobriander fail to see this relation? We would say that it is impossible to have pattern without having elements in relation to one another. These objections are inherent to our own codification of reality. We make them because it is impossible for members of our culture to apprehend being without relationships. We can see motivation only as coming from outside, in relationship, and would therefore say that where we have acts there must be motivation, and where there is motivation relationships must be recognized. Again, we are accustomed to equate change with the dynamic, sameness with the static; and to put these pairs in opposition. So it is hard for us to see that sameness itself can be dynamic. as it is for the Trobriander who does not need "motivation" for his acts, since their very sameness holds value, so that they "motivate" themselves.

These objections raise a further, and a more basic question: is the Trobriander blind to relationships, or are there no relationships? Do we who base our behavior on relationships read these relationships into reality, or are they given? Which codification is true to reality? I would say that the two are not mutually exclusive. They represent different facets of reality and different meaningful phrasings for each culture. The fact that each culture has chosen to base itself on only one aspect does not mean that the other is false. Our peculiar codification makes us blind to other aspects of reality, or makes these meaningless when presented. But one codification does not exhaust reality; neither, if it were false, would a society, I believe, be able to survive with it at its base. The Trobrianders, according to our view of life, should be bored automatons. Actually they act as they want to act, poised and sure, in activities which hold meaning and satisfaction. Whether they are given or read into reality by us, temporality, causation, teleology, and relationship in general have neither meaning nor relevance for Trobriand behavior; but Trobriand behavior is nevertheless good because it is concerned with being; and being, in its appropriate pattern, incorporates value and truth.

REFERENCES

Lee, Dorothy. "A Primitive System of Values." *Philosophy of Science*, 7:355-378 (1940).

Malinowski, Bronislaw. *Argonauts of the Western Pacific*. New York: E. P. Dutton & Co., 1922.

———. *The Sexual Life of the Savages in Northwestern Melanesia*. New York: H. Liveright Publishing Corp., 1929.

———. *Coral Gardens and Their Magic*. New York: American Book Co., 1935.

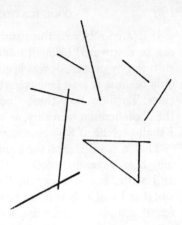

Codifications of Reality:
Lineal and Nonlineal

THE PEOPLE OF THE TROBRIAND IS-
lands codify, and probably apprehend reality, nonlineally in contrast to
our own lineal phrasing. Basic to my investigation of the codification of
reality on these two societies, is the assumption that a member of a given
society not only codifies experienced reality through the use of the specific
language and other patterned behavior characteristics of his culture, but
that he actually grasps reality only as it is presented to him in this code.
The assumption is not that reality itself is relative; rather, that it is differently punctuated and categorized, or that different aspects of it are noticed by, or presented to the participants of different cultures. If reality
itself were not absolute, then true communication of course would be impossible. My own position is that there is an absolute reality, and that
communication is possible. If, then, that which the different codes refer
to is ultimately the same, a careful study and analysis of a different code
and of the culture to which it belongs, should lead us to concepts which
are ultimately comprehensible, when translated into our own code. It may
even, eventually, lead us to aspects of reality from which our own code
excludes us.

From *Psychosomatic Medicine*, May 1950, No. 12.

It is a corollary of this assumption that the specific phrasing of reality can be discovered through intensive and detailed analysis of any aspect of culture. My own study was begun with an analysis of linguistic formulation, only because it is in language that I happen to be best able to discover my clues. To show how these clues can be discovered and used as guides to the apprehension of reality, as well as to show what I mean by codification, I shall present at first concrete material from the field of language.

That a word is not the reality, not the thing which it represents, has long been a commonplace to all of us. The thing which I hold in my hand as I write, *is* not a pencil; I *call* it a pencil. And it remains the same whether I call it *pencil, molyvi, Bleistift,* or *siwiqoq.* These words are different sound-complexes applied to the same reality; but is the difference merely one of sound-complex? Do they refer to the same *perceived* reality? *Pencil* originally meant little tail; it delimited and named the reality according to form. *Molyvi* means lead and refers to the writing element. *Bleistift* refers both to the form and to the writing-element. *Siwiqoq* means painting-stick and refers to observed function and form. Each culture has phrased the reality differently. To say that *pencil,* for example, applies primarily to form is no idle etymologic statement. When we use this word metaphorically, we refer neither to writing element nor to function, but to form alone; we speak of a pencil of light, or a styptic pencil.

When I used the four words for this object, we all knew what reality was referred to; we knew the meaning of the word. We could visualize the object in my hand, and the words all delimited it in the same way; for example, none of them implied that it was a continuation of my fist. But the student of ethnography often has to deal with words which punctuate reality into different phrasings from the ones with which he is familiar. Let us take, for instance, the words for "brother" and "sister." We go to the islands of Ontong Java to study the kinship system. We ask our informant what he calls his sister and he says *ave;* he calls his brother *kainga.* So we equate *ave* with "sister" and *kainga* with "brother." By way of checking our information we ask the sister what she calls her brother; it turns out that for her, *ave* is "brother," not "sister" as we were led to expect; and that it is her sister whom she calls *kainga.*

The same reality, the same actual kinship is present there as with us; but we have chosen a different aspect for naming. We are prepared to account for this; we say that both cultures name according to what we would call a certain type of blood relationship; but whereas we make reference to absolute sex, they refer to relative sex. Further inquiry, however, discloses that in this, also, we are wrong. Because in our own culture we name relatives according to formal definition and biologic relationship, we have thought that this formulation represents reality; and we have tried to understand the Ontong Javanese relationship terms according to these distinctions which, we believe, are given in nature. But the Ontong Javanese classifies relatives according to a different aspect of reality, differently punctuated. And because of this, he applies *kainga* as well to a wife's sister and a husband's brother; to a man's brother's wife and a woman's sister's husband, as well as to a number of other individuals.

Neither sex nor blood relationship, then, can be basic to this term. The Ontong Javanese name according to their everyday behavior and experience, not according to formal definition. A man shares the ordinary details of his living with his brothers and their wives for a large part of the year; he sleeps in the same large room, he eats with them, he jokes and works around the house with them; the rest of the year he spends with his wife's sisters and their husbands, in the same easy companionship. All these individuals are *kainga* to one another. The *ave*, on the other hand, names a behavior of great strain and propriety; it is based originally upon the relative sex of siblings, yes, but it does not signify biologic fact alone. It names a social relationship, a behavior, an emotional tone. *Ave* can never spend their adult life together, except on rare and temporary occasions. They can never be under the same roof alone together, cannot chat at ease together, cannot refer even distantly to sex in the presence of each other, not even to one's sweetheart or spouse; more than that, everyone else must be circumspect when the *ave* of someone of the group is present. The *ave* relationship also carries special obligations toward a female *ave* and her children. *Kainga* means a relationship of ease, full of shared living, of informality, gaiety; *ave* names one of formality, prohibition, strain.

These two cultures, theirs and our own, have phrased and formulated social reality in completely different ways, and have given their formulation different names. The word is merely the name of this specific cultural phrasing. From this one instance we might formulate the hypothesis—a very tentative one—that among the Ontong Javanese names describe emotive experiences, not observed forms or functions. But we cannot accept this as fact, unless further investigation shows it to be implicit in the rest of their patterned behavior, in their vocabulary and the morphology of their language, in their ritual and their other organized activity.

One more instance, this time from the language of the Wintu Indians of California, will deal with the varying aspect or segmentation of experience which is used as a basis of classification. To begin with, we take the stem *muk*. On the basis of this stem we form the word *mukeda*, which means: "I turned the basket bottom up"; we form *mukuhara*, which means: "The turtle is moving along"; and we form *mukurumas*, which means: "automobile." Upon what conceivable principle can an automobile be put in the same category as a turtle and a basket? There is such a principle, however, and it operates also when the Wintu calls the activity of laundering, *to make foam continuously*. According to this principle, he uses only one stem, (puq or poq) to form words for all of the following:

> puqeda: I just pushed a peg into the ground.
> olpuqal: He is sitting on one haunch.
> poqorahara: Birds are hopping along.
> olpoqoyabe: There are mushrooms growing.
> tunpoqoypoqoya: You walk shortskirted,
>   stifflegged ahead of me.

It is difficult for us to discover the common denominator in the different formations from this one stem, or even to believe that there can be one. Yet, when we discover the principle underlying the classification, the categories themselves are understandable. Basic to the classification is the Wintu view of himself as observer; he stays outside the event. He passes no judgment on essence, and where we would have used kinesthetic or participatory experience as the basis of naming, he names as an observer only, for the shape of the activity or the object. The turtle and the automobile can thus naturally be grouped together with the inverted baskets. The mushroom standing on its stem, the fist grasping a peg against the ground, the stiff leg topped by a short skirt or by the body of a bird or of a man resting on a haunch, obviously all belong together in one category. But the progress of a grasshopper cannot be categorized with that of a hopping bird. We, who classify on a different basis, apprehend the hop of the two kinesthetically and see it as basically the same in both cases; but the Wintu see the difference in recurrent shape, which is all-important to them, and so name the two by means of completely different stems. Again, when we discover this principle, it is easy to see that from the observer's point of view laundering is the making of a lot of foam; and to see why, when beer was introduced to the Wintu, it was named *laundry*.

I have discussed at length the diversity of codification of reality in general, because it is the foundation of the specific study which I am about to present. I shall speak of the formulation of experienced reality among the Trobriand Islanders in comparison to our own; I shall speak of the nature of expectancy, of motivation, of satisfaction, as based upon a reality which is differently apprehended and experienced in two different societies; which is, in fact, for each, a different reality. The Trobriand Islanders were studied by the late Bronislaw Malinowski, who has given us the rich and circumstantial material about them which has made this study possible. I have given a detailed presentation of some implications of their language elsewhere; but since it was in their language that I first noticed the absence of lineality, which led me to this study, I shall give here a summary of the implications of the language.

A Trobriand word refers to a self-contained concept. What we consider an attribute of a predicate, is to the Trobriander an ingredient. Where I would say, for example, "A good gardener," or "The gardener is good," the Trobriand word would include both "gardener" and "goodness"; if the gardener loses the goodness, he has lost a defining ingredient, he is something else, and he is named by means of a completely different word. A taytu (a species of yam) contains a certain degree of ripeness, bigness, roundedness, etc.; without one of these defining ingredients, it is something else, perhaps a *bwanawa* or a *yowana*. There are no adjectives in the language; the rare words dealing with qualities are substantivized. The term *to be* does not occur; it is used neither attributively nor existentially, since existence itself is contained; it is an ingredient of being.

Events and objects are self-contained points in another respect; there is a series of beings, but no becoming. There is no temporal connection between objects. The taytu always remains itself; it does not *become* overripe; over-ripeness is an ingredient of another, a different being. At some point, the taytu *turns into a yowana*, which contains over-ripeness. And the yowana, over-ripe as it is, does not put forth shoots, does not *become* a sprouting yowana. When sprouts appear, it ceases to be itself; in its place appears a *silasata*. Neither is there a temporal connection made—or, according to our own premises, perceived—between events; in fact, temporality is meaningless. There are no tenses, no linguistic distinction between past or present. There is no arrangement of activities or events into means and ends, no causal or teleologic relationships. What we consider a causal relationship in a sequence of connected events, is to the Trobriander an ingredient of a patterned whole. He names this ingredient *u'ula*.

There is no automatic relating of any kind in the language. Except for the rarely used verbal it-differents and it-sames, there are no terms of comparison whatever. And we find in an analysis of behavior that the standard for behavior and of evaluation is non-comparative.

These implications of the linguistic material suggest to my mind an absence of axiomatic lineal connection between events or objects in the Trobriand apprehension of reality, and this implication, as I shall attempt to show below, is reinforced in their definition of activity. In our own culture, the line is so basic, that we take it for granted, as given in reality. We see it in visible nature, between material points, and we see it between metaphorical points such as days or acts. It underlies not only our thinking, but also our aesthetic apprehension of the given; it is basic to the emotional climax which has so much value for us, and, in fact, to the meaning of life itself. In our thinking about personality and character, we have taken for granted the presence of the line.

In our academic work, we are constantly acting in terms of an implied line. When we speak of *ap*plying an *at*tribute, for example, we visualize the process as lineal, coming from the outside. If I make a picture of an apple on the board, and want to show that one side is green and the other red I connect these attributes with the pictured apple by means of lines, as a matter of course; how else would I do it? When I organize my data, I *draw* conclusions *from* them. I *trace* a relationship between my facts. I describe a pattern as a *web* of relationships. Look at a lecturer who makes use of gestures; he is constantly making lineal connections in the air. And a teacher with chalk in hand will be drawing lines on the board whether he be a psychologist, a historian, or a paleontologist.

Preoccupation with social facts merely as self-contained facts is mere antiquarianism. In my field, a student of this sort would be an amateur or a dilettante, not an anthropologist. To be an anthropologist, he can arrange his facts in an upward slanting line, in a *unilinear* or *multilinear course* of development; or in *parallel lines* or *converging lines*. Or he may arrange them geographically, with *lines* of diffusion connecting them; or schematically, using *concentric circles*. Or at least, he must indicate what his study *leads to*, what new insights we can *draw from* it. To be accorded status, he must use the guiding line as basic.

The line is found or presupposed in most of our scientific work. It is present in the *induction* and the *deduction* of science and logic. It is present in the philosopher's phrasing of means and ends as lineally connected. Our statistical facts are presented lineally as a *graph* or reduced to a normal *curve*. And all of us, I think, would be lost without our *diagrams*. We *trace* a historical development; we *follow the course* of history and evolution *down* to the present and *up from* the ape; and it is interesting to note, in passing, that whereas both evolution and history are lineal, the first goes up the blackboard, the second goes down.

Our psychologists picture motivation as external, connected with the act through a line, or, more recently, entering the organism through a lineal channel and emerging transformed, again lineally, as response. I have seen lineal pictures of nervous impulses and heartbeats, and with them I have seen pictured lineally a second of time. These were photographs, you will say, of existing fact, of reality; a proof that the line is present in reality. But I am not convinced, perhaps due to my ignorance of mechanics, that we have not created our recording instruments in such a way that they have to picture time and motion, light and sound, heartbeats and nerve impulses lineally, on the unquestioned assumption of the line as axiomatic. The line is omnipresent and inescapable, and so we are incapable of questioning the reality of its presence.

When we see a *line* of trees, or a *circle* of stones, we assume the presence of a connecting line which is not actually visible. And we assume it metaphorically when we follow a *line* of thought, a *course* of action or the *direction* of an argument; when we *bridge* a gap in the conversation, or speak of the *span* of life or of teaching a *course*, or lament our *interrupted career*. We make children's embroidery cards and puzzle cards on this assumption; our performance tests and even our tests for sanity often assume that the line is present in nature and, at most, to be discovered or given visual existence.

But is the line present in reality? Malinowski, writing for members of our culture and using idiom which would be comprehensible to them, described the Trobriand village as follows: "Concentrically with the circular row of yam houses there runs a ring of dwelling huts." He saw, or at any rate, he represented the village as two circles. But in the texts which he recorded, we find that the Trobrianders at no time mention circles or rings or even rows when they refer to their villages. Any word which they use to refer to a village, such as *a* or *this*, is prefixed by the substantival element *kway* which means *bump* or *aggregate of bumps*. This is the element which they use when they refer to a pimple or a bulky rash; or to canoes loaded with yams. In their terms, a village is an aggregate of bumps; are they blind to the circles? Or did Malinowski create the circles himself, out of his cultural axiom?

Again, for us as well as in Malinowski's description of the Trobrianders, which was written necessarily in terms meaningful to us, all effective activity is certainly not a haphazard aggregate of acts, but a lineally planned series of acts leading to an envisioned end. Their gardening with all its specialized activities, both technical and magical, leading to a rich harvest; their *kula* involving the cutting down of trees, the communal dragging of the tree to the beach, the rebuilding or building of large sea-worthy canoes, the provisioning, the magical and ceremonial activities involved—surely ll these can be carried through only if they are lineally conceived.

But the Trobrianders do not describe their activity lineally; they do no dynamic relating of acts; they do not use even so innocuous a connective as *and*. Here is part of a description of the planting of coconut: "Thou-approach-there coconut thou-bring-here-we-plant-coconut thou-go thou-plant our coconut. This-here it-emerge sprout. We-push-away this we-push-away this-other coconut-husk-fiber together sprout it-sit together root." We who are accustomed to seek lineal continuity, cannot help supplying it as we read this; but the continuity is not given in the Trobriand text; and all Trobriand speech, according to Malinowski, is "jerky," given in points, not in connecting lines. The only connective I know of in Trobriand is the *pela* which I mentioned above; a kind of preposition which also means "to jump."

I am not maintaining here that the Trobrianders cannot see continuity; rather that lineal connection is not automatically made by them, as a matter of course. At Malinowski's persistent questioning, for example, they did attempt to explain their activities in terms of cause or motivation, by stating possible "results" of uncooperative action. But Malinowski found their answers confused, self-contradictory, inconsistent; their preferred answer was, "It was ordained of old"—pointing to an ingredient value of the act instead of giving an explanation based on lineal connection.

And when they were not trying to find answers to leading questions, the Trobrianders made no such connection in their speech. They assumed, for example, that the validity of a magical spell lay, not in its results, not in proof, but in its very being; in the appropriateness of its inheritance, in its place within the patterned activity, in its being performed by the appropriate person, in its realization of its mythical basis. To seek validity through proof was foreign to their thinking, yet they attempted to do so at the ethnographer's request. I should add here that their names for constellations imply that here they do see lineal figures; I cannot investigate the significance of this, as I have no contextual material. At any rate, I would like to emphasize that, even if the Trobriander does occasionally supply connecting lines between points, his perception and experience do not automatically fall into a lineal framework.

The fact remains that Trobrianders embark on, what is certainly for us, a series of acts which "must require" planning and purposiveness. They engage in acts of gift-giving and gift-receiving which we can certainly see as an exchange of gifts if we want to. When we plot their journeys, we find that they do go from point to point, they do navigate a course, whether they say so or not. Do they merely refrain from giving linguistic expression to something which they actually recognize in nature? On the nonlinguistic level, do they act on an assumption of a lineality which is given no place in their linguistic formulation?

I believe that, where valued activity is concerned, the Trobrianders do not act on an assumption of lineality at any level. There is organization or rather coherence in their acts because Trobriand activity is patterned activity. One act within this pattern brings into existence a pre-ordained cluster of acts. Perhaps one might find a parallel in our culture in the making of a sweater. When I embark on knitting one, the ribbing at the bottom does not *cause* the making of the neckline, nor of the sleeves or the armholes; and it is not part of a lineal series of acts. Rather it is an indispensable part of a patterned activity which includes all these other acts. Again, when I choose a dress pattern, the acts involved in the making of the dress are already present for me. They are embedded in the pattern which I have chosen.

In this same way, I believe, can be seen the Trobriand insistence that though intercourse is a necessary preliminary to conception, it is not the cause of conception. There are a number of acts in the pattern of procreating; one is intercourse, another the entrance of the spirit of a dead Trobriander into the womb. However, there is a further point here. The Trobrianders, when pressed by the ethnographer or teased by the neighboring Dobuans, showed signs of intense embarrassment, giving the impression that they were trying to maintain unquestioningly a stand in which they had to believe. This, I think, is because pattern is truth and value for them; in fact, acts and being derive value from the embedding pattern.

So the question of the perception of a line remains. It is because they find value in pattern that the Trobrianders act according to nonlineal pattern; not because they cannot perceive lineality.

But all Trobriand activity does not contain value; and when it does not, it assumes lineality, and is utterly despicable. For example, the pattern of sexual intercourse includes the giving of a gift from the boy to the girl; but if a boy gives a gift so as to win the girl's favor, he is despised. Again, the kula pattern includes the eventual reception of a gift from the original recipient; the pattern is such that it keeps the acts physically and temporally completely disparate. In spite of this, however, some men are accused of giving gifts as an inducement to their kula partner to give them a specially good kula gift. Such men are labeled with the vile phrase:

he barters. But this means that, unvalued and despised, lineal behavior does exist. In fact, there are villages in the interior whose inhabitants live mainly by bartering manufactured articles for yams. The inhabitants of Omarakana, about whom Malinowski's work and this study are mainly concerned, will barter with them, but consider them pariahs.

This is to say that it is probable that the Trobrianders experience reality in nonlineal pattern because this is the valued reality; and that they are capable of experiencing lineally, when value is absent or destroyed. It is not to say, however, that this in itself means that lineality is given, is present in nature, and that pattern is not. Our own insistence on the line, such as lineal causality, for example, is also often based on unquestioned belief or value. To return to the subject of procreation, the husband in our culture, who has long hoped, and tried in vain, to beget children, will nevertheless maintain that intercourse causes conception; perhaps with the same stubbornness and embarrassment which the Trobrianders exhibited when maintaining the opposite.

The line in our culture not only connects, but it moves. And as we think of a line as moving from point to point, connecting one to the other, so we conceive of roads as *running from* locality *to* locality. A Trobriander does not speak of roads either as connecting two points, or as *running from* point *to* point. His paths are self-contained, named as independent units; they are not *to* and *from*, they are *at*. And he himself is *at*; he has no equivalent for our *to* or *from*. There is, for instance, the myth of Tudava, who goes—in our view—from village to village and from island to island planting and offering yams. The Trobriand text puts it this way: "Kitava it-shine village already (i.e. completed) he-is-over. 'I-sail I-go Iwa'; Iwa he-anchor he-go ashore . . . He-sail Digumenu . . . They-drive (him off) . . . he-go Kwaywata." Point after point is enumerated, but his sailing from and to is given as a discrete event. In our view, he is actually following a southeasterly course, more or less; but this is not given as course or line, and no directions are even mentioned. In fact, in the several texts referring to journeyings in the Archipelago, no words occur for the cardinal directions. In sailing, the "following" winds are named according to where they are *at*, the place where they strike the canoe, such as wind-striking-the-outrigger-beam; not according to where they *come from*. Otherwise, we find names for the southwest wind (youyo), and the northwest wind (bombatu), but these are merely substantival names which have nothing to do with direction; names for kinds of wind.

When a member of our society gives an unemotional description of a person, he follows an imaginary line, usually downward: from head to foot, from tip to toe, from hair to chin. The Navaho do the opposite, following a line upward. The Trobriander follows no line, at least none that I can see. "My head boils," says a kula spell; and it goes on to enumerate the parts of the head as follows: nose, occiput, tongue, larynx, speech, mouth. Another spell casting a protective fog, runs as follows: "I befog the hand, I befog the foot, I befog the head, I befog the shoulders . . ." There is a magic formula where we do recognize a line, but it is one which Malinowski did not record verbatim at the time, but which he put down later from memory; and it is not improbable that his memory edited the formula according to the lineality of his culture.

When the Trobriander enumerates the parts of a canoe, he does not follow any recognizable lineal order: "Mist . . . surround me my mast . . . the nose of my canoe . . . my sail . . . my steering oar . . . my canoe-gunwale . . . my canoe-bottom . . . my prow . . . my rib . . . my threading-stick . . . my prow-board . . . my transverse stick . . . my canoe-side."

Malinowski diagrams the garden site as a square piece of land subdivided into squares; the Trobrianders refer to it in the same terms as those which they use in referring to a village—a bulky object or an aggregate of bumps. When the plots in the garden site are apportioned to the gardeners, the named plots are assigned by name, the others by location along each named side of the garden. After this, the inner plots, the "belly" of the garden, are apportioned. Following along a physical rim is a procedure which we find elsewhere also. In a spell naming villages on the main island, there is a long list of villages whch lie along the coast northward, then westward around the island, then south. To us, of course, this is lineal order. But we have no indication that the Trobrianders see other than geographical location, point after point, as they move over a physically continuous area; the line as a guide to procedure is not necessarily implied. No terms are used here which might be taken as an implication of continuity; no "along the coast" or "around" or "northward."

When we in our culture deal with events or experiences of the self, we use the line as guide for various reasons, two of which I shall take up here. First, we feel we must arrange events chronologically in a lineal order; how else could our historians discover the causes of a war or a revolution or a defeat? Among the Trobrianders, what corresponds to our history is an aggregate of anecdotes, that is, unconnected points, told without respect to chronological sequence, or development, or causal relationship; with no grammatical distinction made between words referring to past events, or to present or contemplated ones. And in telling an anecdote, they take no care that a temporal sequence should be followed. For instance, they said to Malinowski, "They-eat-taro, they-spew-taro, they-disgusted-taro"; but if time, as we believe, is a moving line, then the revulsion came first in time, the vomiting was the result, coming afterward. Again, they say, "This-here . . . ripes . . . falls-down truly gives-birth . . . sits seed in belly-his"; but certainly the seed is there first, and the birth follows in time, if time is lineal.

Secondly, we arrange events and objects in a sequence which is climactic, in size and intensity, in emotional meaning, or according to some other principle. We often arrange events from earlier to later, not because we are interested in historical causation, but because the present is the climax of our history. But when the Trobriander relates happenings, there is no developmental arrangement, no building up of emotional tone. His stories have no plot, no lineal development, no climax. And when he repeats his garden spell, his list is neither climactic, nor anticlimactic; it sounds merely untidy to us:

> The belly of my garden lifts
> The belly of my garden rises
> The belly of my garden reclines
> The belly of my garden is-a-bushhen's-nest-in-lifting
> The belly of my garden is-an-anthill
> The belly of my garden lifts-bends
> The belly of my garden is-an-ironwood-tree-in-lifting
> The belly of my garden lies-down
> The belly of my garden burgeons.

When the Trobrianders set out on their great ceremonial kula expedition, they follow a pre-established order. First comes the canoe of the Tolab wage, an obscure subclan. Next come the canoes of the great chiefs. But this is not climactic; after the great chiefs come the commoners. The order derives meaning not from lineal sequence, but from correspondence with a present, experienced, meaningful pattern, which is the recreation or realization of the mythical pattern; that which has been ordained of old and is forever. Its meaning does not lie in an item-to-item relationship, but in fitness, in the repetition of an established unit.

An ordering of this sort gives members of our society a certain esthetic dysphoria except when, through deliberate training, we learn to go beyond our cultural expectation; or, when we are too young to have taken on the phrasings of our culture. When we manipulate objects naively, we arrange them on some climactic lineal principle. Think of a college commencement, with the faculty arranged in order of rank or length of tenure or other mark of importance; with the students arranged according to increasing physical height, from shortest to tallest, actually the one absolutely irrelevant principle as regards the completion of their college education, which is the occasion for the celebration. Even when the sophisticated avoid this principle, they are not unconscious of it; they are deliberately avoiding something which is there.

And our arrangement of history, when we ourselves are personally involved, is mainly climactic. My great grandmother sewed by candle light, my grandmother, used a kerosene lamp, my mother did her studying by gaslight, I did it by a naked electric ceiling light, and my children have diffused fluorescent lighting. This is progress; this is the meaningful sequence. To the Trobriander, climax in history is abominable, a denial of all good, since it would imply not only the presence of change, but also that change increases the good; but to him value lies in sameness, in repeated pattern, in the incorporation of all time within the same point. What is good in life is exact identity with all past Trobriand experience, and all mythical experience.

There is no boundary between past Trobriand existence and the present; he can indicate that an action is completed, but this does not mean that the action is past; it may be completed and present or timeless. Where we would say "Many years ago" and use the past tense, the Trobriander will say, "In my father's childhood" and use non-temporal verbs; he places the event situationally, not temporally. Past, present, and future are presented linguistically as the same, are present in his existence, and sameness with what we call the past and with myth, represents value to the Trobriander. Where we see a developmental line, the Trobriander sees a point, at most a swelling in value. Where we find pleasure and satisfaction in moving away from the point, in change as variety or progress, the Trobriander finds it in the repetition of the known, in maintaining the point; that is, in what we call monotony.

Esthetic validity, dignity, and value come to the Trobriander not through arrangement into a climactic line, but rather in the undisturbed incorporation of the events within their original, nonlineal order. The only history which has meaning for him is that which evokes the value of the point, or which, in the repetition, swells the value of the point. For example, every occasion in which a kula object participates becomes an ingredient of its being and swells its value; all these occasions are enumerated with great satisfaction, but the lineal course of the traveling kula object is not important.

As we see our history climactically, so do we plan future experiences climactically, leading up to future satisfaction or meaning. Who but a very young child would think of starting a meal with strawberry shortcake and ending it with spinach? We have come to identify the end of the meal with the height of satisfaction, and we identify semantically the words dessert and reward, only because of the similarity of their position in a climactic line. The Trobriand meal has no dessert, no line, no climax. The special bit, the relish, is eaten *with* the staple food; it is not something to "look *forward to*," while disposing of a meaningless staple.

None of the Trobriand activities is fitted into a climactic line. There is no job, no labor, no drudgery which finds its reward outside the act. All work contains its own satisfaction. We cannot speak of S—R here, as all action contains its own immanent "stimulus." The present is not a means to future satisfaction, but good in itself, as the future is also good in itself; neither better nor worse, neither climactic nor anticlimactic, in fact, not lineally connected nor removed.

It follows that the present is not evaluated in terms of its place within a course of action leading upward to a worthy end. In our culture, we can rarely evaluate the present in itself. I tell you that Sally is selling notions at Woolworth's, but this in itself means nothing. It acquires some meaning when I add that she has recently graduated from Vassar. However, I go on to tell you that she has been assistant editor of *Vogue*, next a nursemaid, a charwoman, a public school teacher. But this is a mere jumble; it makes no sense and has no meaning, because the series leads to nothing. You cannot relate one job to another, and you are unable to see them discretely simply as part of her being. However, I now add that she is gathering material for a book on the working mother. Now all this falls in line, it makes sense in terms of a career. Now her job is good and it makes her happy, because it is part of a planned climactic line leading to more pay, increased recognition, higher rank. There was a story in a magazine about the college girl who fell in love with the milkman one summer; the reader felt tense until it was discovered that this was just a summer job, that it was only a means for the continuation of the man's education in the Columbia Law School. Our evaluation of happiness and unhappiness is bound with this motion along an envisioned line leading to a desired end. In the fulfillment of this course or career—not in the fulfillment of the self as point—do we find value. Our conception of freedom rests on the principle of non-interference with this moving line, non-interruption of the intended course of action.

It is difficult to tell whether climax is given in experience at all, or whether it is always imposed on the given. At a time when progress and evolution were assumed to be implicit in nature, our musicians and writers gave us climactic works. Nowadays, our more reflective art does not present experience climactically. Then, is emotion itself climactic? Climax, for us, evokes "thrill" or "drama." But we have cultures, like the Tikopia, where life is lived, to our perception, on an even emotive plane without thrill or climax. Experiences which "we know to be" climactic, are described without climax by them. For example, they, as well as the Trobrianders, described intercourse as an aggregate of pleasurable experiences. But Malinowski is disturbed by this; he cannot place the erotic kiss in Trobriand experience, since it has no climactic function.

In our culture, childbearing is climactic. Pregnancy is represented by the usual obstetrician as an uncomfortable means to a dramatic end. For most women, all intensity of natural physical experience is nowadays removed from the actual birth itself; but the approach of birth nevertheless is a period of mounting tension, and drama is supplied by the intensive social recognition of the event, the dramatic accumulation of gifts, flowers, telegrams. A pregnancy is not formally announced since, if it does not eventuate in birth, it has failed to achieve its end; and failure to reach the climax brings shame. In its later stages it may be marked with a shower; but the shower looks forward to the birth, it does not celebrate the pregnancy itself. Among the Trobrianders, pregnancy has meaning in itself, as a state of being. At a first pregnancy, there is a long ceremonial involving "preparatory" work on the part of many people, which merely celebrates the pregnancy. It does not anchor the baby, it does not *have as its purpose* a more comfortable time during the pregnancy, it does not *lead to* an easier birth or a healthy baby. It makes the woman's skin white, and makes her be at her most beautiful; yet this *leads to* nothing, since she must not attract men, not even her own husband.

Are we then right in accepting without question the presence of a line in reality? Are we in a position to say with assurance that the Trobrianders are wrong and we are right? Much of our present-day thinking, and much of our evaluation, are based on the premise of the line and of the line as good. Students have been refused admittance to college because the autobiographic sketch accompanying their application showed absence of the line; they lacked purposefulness and ability to plan; they were inadequate as to character as well as intellectually. Our conception of personality formation, our stress on the significance of success and failure and of frustration in general, is based on the axiomatically postulated line. Yet can there be blocking without presupposed lineal motion or effort? If I walk along a path because I like the country, or if it is not important to get to a particular point at a particular time, then the insuperable puddle from the morning's shower is not frustrating; I throw stones into it and watch the ripples, and then choose another path. If the undertaking is of value in itself, a point good in itself, and not because it leads to something, then failure has no symbolic meaning; it merely results in no cake for supper, or less money in the family budget; it is not personally destructive. But failure is devastating in our culture, because it is not failure of the undertaking alone; it is the moving, becoming, lineally conceived self which has failed.

Ethnographers have occasionally remarked that the people whom they studied showed no annoyance when interrupted. Is this an indication of mild temper, or might it be the case that they were not interrupted at all, as there was no expectation of lineal continuity? Such questions are new in anthropology and most ethnographers therefore never thought of recording material which would answer them. However, we do have enough material to make us question the line as basic to all experience; whether it is actually present in given reality or not, it is not always present in experienced reality. We cannot even take it for granted as existing among those members of our society who are not completely or naively steeped in their culture, such as many of our artists, for example. And we should be very careful, in studying other cultures, to avoid the unexamined assumption that their actions are based on the predication of a lineal reality.

REFERENCES

Being and Value in a Primitive Culture. Journal of Philosophy 46:401-415 (1949). See references under *Being and Value in a Primitive Culture.*

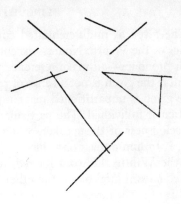

Linguistic Reflection
of Wintu Thought

A BASIC TENET OF THE WINTU LAN-
guage, expressed both in nominal and verbal categories, is that reality—
ultimate truth—exists irrespective of man. Man's experience actualizes
this reality, but does not otherwise affect its being. Outside man's experience, this reality is unbounded, undifferentiated, timeless.

In fact, if "existence" and "being" are seen as referring to history, to
the here and now, then this reality cannot be said to exist, and the Wintu
certainly do not assert its existence or being. Yet I must apply these terms
to it, since I have to use the English language. Man believes it but does
not know it. He refers to it in his speech but does not assert it; he leaves
it untouched by his senses, inviolate. Within his experience, the reality
assumes temporality and limits. As it impinges upon his consciousness he
imposes temporary shape upon it. Out of the undifferentiated qualities
and essences of the given reality, he individuates and particularizes, im-
pressing himself diffidently and transiently, performing acts of will with
circumspection. Matter and relationships, essence, quality are all given.
The Wintu actualizes a given design endowing it with temporality and
form through his experience. But he neither creates nor changes; the de
sign remains immutable.

From *International Journal of American Linguistics*, 1944, Vol. 10.

The given as undifferentiated content is implicit in the nominal categories of the Wintu. Nouns—except for kinship terms, which are classified with pronouns—all make reference primarily to generic substance. To the Wintu, the given is not a series of particulars, to be classed into universals. The given is unpartitioned mass; a part of this the Wintu delimits into a particular individual. The particular then exists, not in nature, but in the consciousness of the speaker. What to us is a class, a plurality of particulars, is to him a mass or a quality or an attribute. These concepts are one for the Wintu; the word for *red*, for example, is the same as for *redness* or *red-mass*. Plurality, on the other hand, is not derived from the singular and is of slight interest to him. He has no nominal plural form, and when he does use a plural word, such as *men*, he uses a root which is completely different from the singular word; *man* is wita but *men* is gis.

To someone brought up in the Indo-European tradition, this is a position hard to understand. We know that the plural is derived from the singular. It is logical and natural for our grammars to start with the singular form of a noun or a verb, and then go on to the plural. When we are faced with words like group or herd or flock, we call them, as a matter of course, collective plurals. Words like sheep or deer, which make no morphological distinction between singular and plural, are explained on the basis of historical accident or the mechanics of enunciation. But to the Wintu it is natural to speak of deer or salmon without distinction of number; to him a flock is a whole, not a collection of singular individuals. To us, the distinction of number is so important that we cannot mention an object unless we also simultaneously indicate whether it is singular or plural; and if we speak of it in the present tense, the verb we use must echo this number. And the Greek had to do more than this; if he had to make a statement such as *the third man who entered was old and blind,* the words *third, who entered, was, old* and *blind,* though referring to nonquantitative concepts, all had to reiterate the singularity of the man. The Wintu, on the other hand, indicates number only if he, the speaker, chooses to do so. In such a case he can qualify his noun with a word such as *many* or *one*; or he can express plurality of object or subject through special forms of the verb.

The care which we bestow on the distinction of number is lavished by the Wintu on the distinction between particular and generic. But here is a further difference. Whereas we find number already present in substance itself, the Wintu imposes particularity upon substance. We *must* use a plural when we are confronted by plural objects; the Wintu *chooses* to use a particularizing form. It is true that for certain nouns, such as

those referring to live people and animals, the Wintu uses a particularizing form almost always; that for substances which we also regard as generic,
such as fire and sand and wood, he almost always uses a generic form.
But these are merely habitual modes of speaking from which he can and
does deviate.

His distinction, then, is subjective. He starts from *whiteness* or *white*
(hayi) a quality, and derives from this, as an observer, the particular—the
white one (hayit). With the use of derivative suffixes, he delimits a part
of the mass. We take the word for *deer* for example. In the instances I
give, I shall use only the objective case, nop for the generic, and the nopum
for the particular. A hunter went out but saw no *deer*, nop; another killed
a *deer*, nopum. A woman carried *deer*, nop, to her mother; a hunter
brought home *deer*, nopum. Now the woman's deer was cut in pieces and
carried, a formless mass, in her back-basket; but the man carried his two
deer slung whole from his shoulder. Some brothers were about to eat venison; they called, "Old man, come and eat *venison*, (nop)." The old man
replied, "You can eat that stinking *venison*, (nopum) yourselves." The
brothers saw it just as deer meat; to the old man it was the flesh of a particular deer, one which had been killed near human habitation, fed on
human offal.

I have recorded two versions of the same tale, told respectively by a
man and a woman. The man refers to a man's weapons and implements
in the particular; the woman mentions them all as generic. The use of
the word sem (se) is illuminating in this connection. As generic, sem,
it means *hand* or *both hands* of one person, the fingers merged in one
mass; spread out the hand, and now you have delimited parts of the hand:
semum, *fingers*.

For the Wintu, then, essence or quality is generic and found in nature;
it is permanent and remains unaffected by man. Form is imposed by man,
through act of will. But the impress man makes is temporary. The deer
stands out as an individual only at the moment of man's speech; as soon
as he ceases speaking, the deer merges into deerness.

The concept of the immutability of essence and the transiency of form,
of the fleeting significance of delimitation, is reflected in Wintu mythology. Matter was always there; the creator, *He who is above*, a vague
being, was really a Former. People do not *come into being* as I say in my
faulty literal translation of the myths; they *grow out of the ground*; they
always existed. Dawn and daylight, fire and obsidian have always been in
existence, hoarded; they are finally stolen and given a new role. In the
myths, various characters *form* men out of materials which are already

present; Coyote, for example, changes sticks into men. Throughout, form is shifting and relatively unimportant.

The characters, Coyote, Buzzard, Grizzly Bear, etc., are bewilderingly men and animals in their attributes, never assuming stable form. Even this semi-defined form may be changed with ease; Grosbeak is steamed faultily, for example, and turns into a grasshopper. The Wintu speak of these characters in English as *Coyote, Loon,* not *a coyote.* We have assumed that by this they mean a proper name. But it is probable that they refer to something undelimited, as we, for example, distinguish between fire and a fire. These characters die and reappear in another myth without explanation. They become eventually the coyotes and grizzly bears we know, but not through a process of generation. They are a prototype, a genus, a quality which, however, is not rigidly differentiated from other qualities.

The premise of primacy of the whole finds expression in the Wintu concept of himself as originally one, not a sum of limbs or members. When I asked for a word for the body I was given the term *the whole person.* The Wintu does not say *my head aches;* he says *I head ache.* He does not say *my hands are hot;* he says *I hands am hot.* He does not say *my leg,* except extremely rarely and for good reason, such as that his leg has been severed from his body. The clothes he wears are part of this whole. A Wintu girl does not say *her dress was striped* but *she was dress striped.* In dealing with the whole, the various aspects referred to are generic; only when particularization is necessary as a device to distinguish toes or fingers from feet and hands is it used. But when the leg is not part of the whole, when the subject is cutting out the heart of a victim, then particularization is used, since the activity is seen from the point of view of the subject. And when a woman is ironing her dress, which is not part of her body any more, she refers to it as something separate: *my dress.*

In his verbal phrase, the Wintu shows himself again humble in the face of immutable reality, but not paralyzed into inactivity. Here again he is faced with being which is, irrespective of himself, and which he must accept without question. A limited part of this comes within his ken; his consciousness, cognition, and sensation act as a limiting and formalizing element upon the formless reality. Of this delimited part he speaks completely in terms of the bounds of his own person. He uses a stem, derived from the primary root, which means *I know,* or *this is within experience.*

The definitive suffixes (in parentheses below) which he uses with this convey, in every case, the particular source of his information, the particular aspect of himself through which he has become cognizant of what he states.

The material he presents has become known to him through his eyes,— 'the child is playing (-be) in the sand'; or through his other senses—'this is sour (nte)' or 'he is yelling (-nte)'; or through his logic—'he is hungry (-el; he must be hungry since he has had no food for two days)'; or through the action of logic upon the circumstantial evidence of the senses —'a doe went by with two fawns (-re; I see their tracks)'; or through his acceptance of hearsay evidence—'they fought long (-ke; someone told me).' In this category of experience, the future is stated in terms of in tention or desire or attempt. This is a future which depends on an act of will and is not stated with certainty. This is the aspect of experience with which the unreflective among us concern themselves exclusively; as one of my students asked: 'And what is left outside?'

Outside is the reality which is beyond personal cognition, a reality which is accepted in faith. For this, the Wintu uses the primary form of the verb. Alone this stem forms a command; yoqu means *wash!* (*you must wash,*) a reference to given necessity. With the aid of different suffixes, this stem may refer to a timeless state, as when setting given conditions for a certain activity; or to what we call the passive, when the individual does not par ticipate as a free agent. In general, it refers to the not-experienced and not-known. To this stem is appended the non-assertive -mina, and the resulting verbal form contains, then, potentially both positive and nega tive alternatives simultaneously. With the proper auxiliaries, this may either be used to negate, or to ask a question requiring a yes-or-no answer; or in phrases implying ignorance; but it can never assert the known. And when a Wintu gives a negative command, he uses this form again; he does not say 'don't chop' but *may it remain* (bedi) *unactualized-chop* (kop mina).

To this not-experienced, timeless, necessary reality, the Wintu refers chiefly in terms of natural necessity; by means of one suffix, -les, (a nomi nal form of -le) he refers to a future that must be realized, to a probability which is at the same time potential, necessary and inevitable. Words modified by this suffix, are translated by the Wintu variously with the aid of *may,* or *might,* or *would,* or *must,* or *can* or *shall.* Another reference to this reality is made with the aid of the unmodified -le. This suffix can be used with personal suffixes, to indicate a future of certainty, in the realiza tion of which the subject does not participate as a free agent. It is a future so certain, that this form, also, is sometimes translated with *must;* for example, "You, too, shall die." Without personal endings, the -le ties to gether two events or states of being in inevitable sequence, with no refer ence to specific time. The sequence may be translated by the Wintu with the aid of the purposive *so as to*, or *to* or with *about to*, but there is no subjective purpose involved; or the word *before* may be used in the translation.

Now the -le refers to a succession of events in nature, and to an inevitable sequence. But here the Wintu can act of his own free will and decide on one of the members of the sequence. He can interpolate an act of choice and thus bring about a desired sequence. Or the subject can intercept an undesirable sequence, by changing the first unit. The same stem is used for this, but a different suffix -ken (second person), which the Wintu translates either as *so that you should not*, or *you might* or *don't*; that is, the suffix warns of the pending sequence, and implies: avoid it. For example, a man shouts to his daughter who is standing on a ladder, *Be careful, you might fall off* or *don't fall off* (talken). Someone instructs two boys: sight carefully when you shoot, *so as not to miss*, or *you might miss*, or *don't miss* (manaken). And a woman, who hears that a rattlesnake has been seen near the water, says, 'Let me not go swimming; I *might get stung* (toptcukida).' Pia ihkedi (*he might do it himself*, or *don't let him do it*, is, according to my informant, equivalent to saying, 'you'd better do it yourself.' So the role of the Wintu in the future is not creative, but can be formative, *i.e.*, it is either negative, or takes the form of an interpolation between necessary events. Here, again the act of will exists, but appears limited to a choice between actualizing and refraining from actualizing.

It is impossible to tell to what extent the reluctance to penetrate beyond external form is active in the formation of words. If the Wintu offers me an English word in translation for a Wintu one, I rarely have any way of knowing what exactly the word means to him. When he says that watca is to *weep*, for example, is he, like me, thinking of the whole kinesthetic activity with all its emotional implications, or is he merely concerned with the sound of keening, as I think he is? Whenever I find a group of words derived from the same root, I can clearly see that they point to a preoccupation with form alone. I find in my glossary a word for *to shave the head* (poyoqteluna) for example. There is no reason to question the English rendering till I examine the root from which it is derived. I find other derivatives from this root. One means: to *pull off a scab*; another *to have a damp forehead*. If there is to be a common meaning the first is not concerned with the activity of prying off a scab, or with the sensation of the skin; it refers only to the glistening skin exposed. Neither is the second concerned with the sensation of dampness, but, again, merely with the appearance of the skin. So, though the Wintu uses *to shave the head* as the equivalent to poyoqteluna, I am concerned rather with the activity of cutting itself, with the feel of the scalp, the complete removal of hair, whereas the Wintu refers only to the way the end result appears to the observer; his word means *to make one's own scalp glisten*.

I have recorded a word which applies to the pounding of non-brittle objects. I have translated it as *to pound to a pulp*. I have passed judgment as to what happens to the consistency of the buckeye when I pound it. But the Wintu is merely making a statement as to the external form of the pounded mass; from this word *tira*, he derives his word for terus, *tick*.

The same insistence upon outward form alone has influenced the naming of White traits. Where I say *he plays the piano*, the Wintu says *he makes a braying noise*. I name the automobile after its locomotion, an essential aspect of its being. But the Wintu in his preoccupation with form alone, finds no incongruity in classifying the automobile with the turtle as: *that which looks like an inverted pot in motion*.

Especially illustrative of this attitude are the words tlitiq and -lila, which the Wintu uses in situations where we would have used *make, create, manufacture*; or, more colloquially, *fix*. But these English equivalents are far from the meaning of the Wintu words; -lila, which I have often translated as *manufacture*, actually means *to turn into, to transform*; that is, to change one form into another. And tlitiq does not mean *make*; it means *to work on*. Our *make* often implies creation, the tlitiq finds matter, assumes its presence. *Make* presupposes an act of aggression, the imposition of self upon matter; tlitiq also involves an act of will but one which is restrained and spends itself on the surface.

This respect for the inviolability of the given finds further expression in the conception of the relationship between self and other. Two Wintu suffixes, which in English are rendered as coercive, reflect this attitude. One of these is -il or -wil, used to make a verb transitive, when the object is particular. For example, tipa means *to cross* (a river or ridge); tepuwil means *to take across* (a child, beads, weapons, etc.). But the -il may also mean *to do with*; so that tepuwil may mean *to go across with*. There is the term bewil which means *to possess something particular*; but it also means *to be with*. The initiative is with the subject in both cases; but there is no act of aggression; there is a coordinate relationship. The word sukil, applied to a chief, I have translated as *to rule*; but the word means *to stand with*. We would say, at best, that the suffix has the two meanings at the same time; but the Wintu makes no distinction between the two concepts, except when he has to use a language which reflects a habit of thought that regards this distinction as natural.

Another suffix which, like the -il, deals with the relationship of self and other, is -ma. This sometimes appears as a causative; for example, ba means *to eat* and bama means *to feed*, that is, *to give to eat, to make eat.* Pira means *to swallow;* peruma *to fish with bait.* But like the -il this too implies a coordinate relationship, and one of great intimacy between self and other; for example a chief tells his people: (*with the coming* of the Whites) *you shall hunger*—biralebosken, *your children shall hunger*—biramalebosken (literally *children you shall hunger in respect of*). The relatives of a pubescent girl -bahlas—are referred to as bahlmas (*they were pubescent in respect of*). A man says, koyumada ilam; kuya is *to be ill;* the man says in effect *I am ill in respect to my child.* I use *in respect to* for an other which is not entirely separated from the self, and with which the self is intimately concerned. What we express as an act of force, is here expressed in terms of continuity between self and other.

I have avoided advisedly the use of the term identification here. This term implies an original delimitation and separation. It is the nearest that our social scientists, starting from delimitation, can come to unity. But if the Wintu starts with an original oneness, we must speak, not of identification, but of a premise of continuity.

We find this premise underlying, not only linguistic categories, but his thought and behavior throughout. It is basic to the Wintu attitude toward society, for example. It explains why kinship terms are classified, not with the substantives, but with the pronouns such as *this;* why the special possessives used with them, such as the net, in nettan *my father,* are really pronouns of participation, to be used also with aspects of one's identity as, for example, my act, my intention, my future death. To us, in the words of Ralph Linton, 'society has as its foundation an aggregate of individuals.' For the Wintu, the individual is a delimited part of society; it is society that is basic, not a plurality of individuals. Again, this premise of the primacy of the unpartitioned whole gives a valid basis to beliefs such as that a man will lose his hunting luck if he goes on a hunt while his wife is menstruating. Where formal distinctions are derivative and transitory, a man is at one with his wife in a way which is difficult if not impossible for us to appreciate.

There is further the Wintu premise of a reality beyond his delimiting experience. His experience is that of a reality as shaped by his perception and conceptualization. Beyond it is the timeless design to which his experience has given temporality. He believes in it, and he taps it through his ritual acts and his magic, seeking "luck" to reinforce and validate his experiential skills and knowledge, to endow his acts with effectiveness. A hunter must have both skill and luck; but skill is the more limited. An unskilled hunter who has luck, can still hit a deer by rare chance, but a skilled hunter without luck can never do so. The myths contain examples of hunters who, having lost their luck, can never kill a deer again. Now knowledge and skill are phrased agentively and experientially; but luck is phrased passively or in terms of non-actualized reality. The hunter who has lost his luck does not say *I cannot kill deer any more*, but *Deer don't want to die for me.*

The natural, reached through luck, is impersonal; it cannot be known or sensed, and it is never addressed; but not so the supernatural. It can be felt or seen; it is personal. It is within experience. Such experience can be questioned and proof of it is often offered; the doctoring shaman produces as evidence the fish he has extracted from a patient, the missile of some supernatural being. Klutchie, a shaman, offers his knowledge of a coast language as proof that, during a protracted trance of which he has no memory, he was carried by a spirit to the West Coast. But natural necessity is beyond question, and demands no proof. It is only implied; there is no name for it. The supernatural is named and can be spoken of. Toward the supernatural the Wintu performs acts of will. The shaman, speaking to the spirit he controls, will command and demand. But the man who dives deep into a sacred pool to seek luck, will say *May it happen that I win at gambling.* His request is non-agentive and impersonal; he does not address nature, neither does he command.

Recurring through all this is the attitude of humility and respect toward reality, toward nature and society. I cannot find an adequate English term to apply to a habit of thought which is so alien to our culture. We are aggressive toward reality. We say, This is bread; we do not say like the Wintu, *I call this bread*, or *I feel* or *taste* or *see it to be bread*. The Wintu never says starkly *this is*; if he speaks of reality which is not within his own restricting experience, he does not affirm it, he only implies it. If he speaks of his experience, he does not express it as categorically true. Our attitude toward nature is colored by a desire to control and exploit. The Wintu relationship with nature is one of intimacy and mutual courtesy. He kills a deer only when he needs it for his livelihood, and utilizes every part of it, hoofs and marrow and hide and sinew and flesh. Waste is abhorrent to him, not because he believes in the intrinsic virtue of thrift, but because the deer had died for him. A man too old to fend for himself prays:

. . . I cannot go up to the mountains in the west to you,
deer;
I cannot kill you and bring you home . . .
You, water, I can never dip you up and fetch you home again . . .
You who are wood, you wood, I cannot carry you home on
my shoulder.

This is not the speech of one who has plucked the fruits of nature by brute force; it is the speech of a friend.

REFERENCES

DuBois, Cora. *Wintu Ethnography*. University of California Publications in American Archaeology and Ethnology, 36, 1935.

Lee, Dorothy. "Some Indian Texts Dealing with the Supernatural." *The Review of Religion*, May, 1944.

See references under: *The Conception of Self Among the Wintu.*

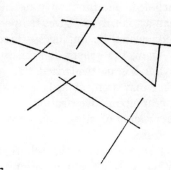

The Conception of the Self
Among the Wintu Indians

THE WINTU INDIANS OF NORTHERN CAL-
ifornia have a conception of the self which is markedly different from our
own. I have attempted to arrive at this conception through an intensive
analysis of linguistic form and structure, as well as a consideration of bio-
graphical texts and recorded mythical material. My study is incomplete,
since I have no other record of actual behavior. The ethnography of the
Wintu as we have it, is an account of a dead and remembered culture. As
a background to the Wintu material, I present occasionally linguistic clues
to our own conception of the self.

The definition of the self in our own culture rests on our law of contradiction. The self cannot be both self and not self, both self and other;
the self excludes the other. Wintu philosophy in general has no law of
contradiction. Where we have mutually exclusive dualistic categories, the
Wintu have categories which are inclusive, but not mutually so; that is,
object A will be included in object B, but not vice versa. Out of this context, B can be distinguished or emphasized through various linguistic devices. For example, in Wintu thought, man is included in nature; natural
law, timeless order, is basic and true, irrespective of man. However, in-

From *Journal of Abnormal and Social Psychology*, No. 3, 1950, Vol. 45.

dependent judgment, private experience and free will are not thereby excluded, but function transiently within the framework of natural law; man actualizes and gives temporality and concreteness to the natural order upon which he impinges—through act of will and personal intent. Again, the generic is primary to the particular and includes it; the individual is particularized transiently, but is not set in opposition. And what may seem at first encounter to be suffixes of mutual exclusiveness, appear upon investigation to be different kinds of emphatics. Even the equivalents of *either* and *or* are emphatics, presupposing inclusiveness or increase.

The concept of the self forms one of these non-exclusive categories. When speaking about Wintu culture, we cannot speak of the self *and* society, but rather of the self *in* society. As a member of my society, writing for readers of this cultural background, I am presenting my study from the point of view of the self and its gradually decreasing participation in society; however, I believe that this is only due to my cultural bias, and that a Wintu would have started from what for us is the opposite direction, the gradual distinguishing of the self from society.

In our own culture, we are clear as to the boundaries of the self. In our commonly held unreflective view, the self is a distinct unit, something we can name and define. We know what is the self and what is not the self; and the distinction between the two is always the same. With the Wintu, the self has no strict bounds, is not named and is not, I believe, recognized as a separate entity.

There are words which deal with the self alone. I do not include among them the *ni: I*, since this is completely dependent for its meaning on the conception of the self held by the speaker who is using it. There are, however, verbs dealing with being or activities and other experiences of the self. For example, we have *limelda: ail-I*. This clearly refers to the self. But what does *tutuhum limtcada:* mother *ail(tca)-I*, or *sukuyum limtcada:* dog *ail(tca)-I* refer to? Which is self and which is other here? The phrases mean, in our terms: my mother is ill, or my dog is ill; but the Wintu is not referring to a distinct, related other, but rather to an other in which he is involved. Actually, this phrasing is used only when speaking of intimates; it is also possible—but I do not know how common—to say in so many words: my mother ails.

Our own linguistic usage through the years, reveals a conception of an increasingly assertive, active and even aggressive self, as well as of an increasingly delimited self. In Chaucer's English, we find the reflection of a way of thinking where events happened to the self much more often than our own usage implies. In Chaucer we find: "it reweth *me*,' 'thus dreamed *me*,' 'melikes" and 'himlikode'; but we say now: *I* rue, *I* dream, *I* like.

Not only do we think of ourselves as actors here, but we phrase this 'activity" as directed at a distinct other. When I say: I like him, I cast my statement into the subject-to-object-affected mold; I imply that I have done something to him. Actually, he may be totally ignorant of my liking and unaffected; only I myself am certainly and directly affected by it.

Over the years, the English language has followed an analytic and isolating trend and it is possible that in linguistic reference there has been an increasing separation of the self from the encompassing situation. At any rate, delimitation of the self is reflected in our increasing analysis of holistic Anglo-Saxon terms referring to bodily acts. I *beckon* is becoming literary or at least cultivated; I *gape* is being replaced by phrases such as: with my mouth open. I say: *I* shake *my* fist, *I* bump *my* head; and how much is left of *me*, the self?

Our language implies not only that the self is narrowly delimited, but that it is also in control. *My* is the pronoun which we call possessive, whose distinguishing characteristic, we are told, is that of possession or ownership; and possession in our culture means control: mine, to do with as I wish. And *my* is a word very frequently used. It is difficult to say what exactly is this self which is delimited and in control. We say: my time, my life—in the sense of *zoe* as well as of *bios*—my experience, my consciousness, my reason, my emotions, my identity. As far as the physical aspect is concerned, there seems to be a central point to which the *my* refers the various fragments. We say: I lift my foot, but there is no such relationship between hand and foot; I cannot say: my hand lifts its foot. The two are referred to the self; they are related only through the self and are both subordinate to the self. But the self is not identified with the physical aspect of the individual. *I* am also in control of *my* body, which I dress, I adorn, I abuse.

When it comes to the non-physical aspects, we note a reflection of the dualism of mind and matter and the hierarchy which is a corollary of this. 'Passions are considered lower: I *fall* in love, I *fall* into a passion or a rage. I delve into my unconscious, which is implicitly underneath; but I analyze my conscious, where I do not need to excavate, since it is on my level. I lose and recover my consciousness or my reason; I never *fall* into consciousness or reason. Neither do I control my will; I exercise it. The self is most nearly identified with consciousness and reason and will; and in our culture, reason and will power and consciousness—particularly self-consciousness—spell mastery and control. So here, too, we find the implication that the self is in control of the other.

Wintu has no such fragmenting. When I asked my Wintu informant Sadie Marsh what the word for *body* was, she said *kot wintu,* the whole person. To the Wintu a person is holistic; he is psychosomatic, but without the suggestion of synthesis which this term holds. They have no word for body or corpse, and the so-called parts of the body are aspects or locations. Neither do they have a word for the self. In English, the word has a long history; and the compounds *myself* and *yourself* were in use by the fourteenth century. The Wintu language does not show the presence of a concept of an established separate self; but the Wintu can emphasize one 'self,' and through the use of grammatical devices he can distinguish an individual at will. The suffix *'a* added to *pi:* he, means *he himself; yoken* added to *pi* means *he alone.* The suffix *ken,* added to a name or other noun emphasizes the individual referred to in contrast to all other individuals who have been included in the expectation. For example, *Sadieken hina* means: *Sadie-of-all-those-expected has-come.*

A study of the grammatical expression of identity, relationship and otherness, shows that the Wintu conceive of the self not as strictly delimited or defined, but as a concentration, at most, which gradually fades and gives place to the other. Most of what is other for us, is for the Wintu completely or partially or upon occasion, identified with the self. For example, the Wintu do not use *and* when referring to individuals who are, or live or act together. Instead of analyzing the *we* into: *John and I,* they say *John we,* using the John as a specification. Only when two individuals who are not already in relatedness are brought together, is the *and* used.

Quite often relatives are referred to in terms of the plural of togetherness. For example: *sohapulel pel: sibling*—(verb)—*together the-two:* the two who sibling-together, i.e. he and his sister; *sedet pel putahtchupulel bos: coyote they-two grandmother-together lived; yoqupulel: wash together* or *wash each other.* Notice that except for the *soha,* the relationship presented is inherently one-directional, so that the togetherness is viewed from one point of view. In the example representing an activity, the *pulel* can be seen as referring to mutuality; but I think that this is a concept introduced from our own culture. In most cases what we find is spatial and temporal concurrence; for example: *ilawi watchupurebinte: the babies are (all) crying together* (according to my hearing); *bolpurun piterum tchuhpure: drink-together-while they gambled-together.*

As with us, the being or existence of the self and activities of the self in process, are expressed as identical with the self; though our own usage,

which separates the person from the verb implies some separation. So in
I go, the ego is separated from its own activity, *go*. The Wintu says *harada:*
I go, or *we go*, in one unanalyzed word, and uses *ni* (I) or *niterum* (we)
only if he wishes to, by way of clarification or denotation. He uses exactly
the same form when he refers to a part of the body, or even to the clothing
which he has on; for example, *I-go-weak legs: my legs are growing weak.*
A Wintu will say: *face-I-am-red*, where face refers to place or aspect of the
whole person. He will say: *you-are-ripped-clothes*, or *you-are-pretty-dress-
striped*; and *nose-run-I* or *arm-broke-I*. Unlike us, a Wintu self is identical
with the parts of his body and is not related to them as other, so long as
they are physically part of him. But when a hair has fallen off his head, it
is *his* hair, when a heart has been plucked out of a man it is *his* heart,
when a man has cut off his arm it is *his* arm; and when a woman is folding
her dress it is *her* dress. When they are physically separated, they are related to him.

When a Wintu performs an act whose consequences revert upon himself, he uses a suffix, *-na*. He phrases holistically, what we phrase in terms
of reversion to the self as a grammatical object. We say, *I feel* (cold) and,
I feel myself (with my hands); i.e., *I* is stated as separate from the self.
The Wintu says *muteda, I-feel*, and *mutnada: I-feel-myself.*

There are two other suffixes, which also imply a certain degree of otherness in which the individual participates coordinately, or in which he is
otherwise involved. The suffix *ma* represents thinking which runs counter
to our own, and was very difficult for me to understand. For a long time
I considered it a causative; *ba*, for example, I translated as *to eat*, and
bama as to *feed, to cause to eat*; *peru* means *to swallow* and *peruma:* to
fish with bait; *taqiq* means *to hurt* and *taqiqmabinte* means *she made me
hurt* (I feel). This was all clearly causative. However, the weight of the
accumulated obscure exceptions finally overpowered my rule. For example,
I found phrases such as the following:

> *applum hesihamada: apples pithy-ma-am.* Yet I have not caused my apples
> to be pithy; in fact, Sadie, who said this, had just bought the apples.

> *hlalmas nis ibesken: stink me you-are:* (*hlal* means to stink and *mas* is the
> second person of *ma*) *you think that I stink.*

> kot bahlmastot . . . *tchuqpure: all menstruating-for-the-first-time-ma-these*
> . . . *helped together;* i.e., all the relatives of the pubescent girl helped;
> this was said of the male relatives of the pubescent girl.

To make the *ma* comprehensible to members of our society, we have to
translate it either as a causative or as adverb-forming. For example, *tchala*

means *to be good* or *nice*, and *tchaluma* means *to do well* or *do carefully*; *tcaluma i!* means *be careful!* Then, tepumas *tchalumatchupumada:* (my) *garden nicely grow*-ma-*am*, may be translated as: I made my garden grow nicely, or: I am doing well in respect to my garden. Primary in the *ma* is the implication of involvement or participation; this may be interpreted by us as a continuity of participation in another state or act (i.e., as an adverb), or as manipulative. I cannot tell whether these different meanings are present for the Wintu; Sadie told me that *tchupumada* did not necessarily imply that I was taking care of my garden. I think the implication of control is absent from the suffix.

The other suffix, il, also appears to express aggressive action, at first encounter. In our own phrasing, whereas *ma* could be manipulative (to get him to do), *il* would be out and out aggressive; *il* would be translated as: to do to. So, *wer* means *to come*, and *weril, to bring; pile* means *to wind*, and *hunpilewil* means *bound him up*. But then we also have: *put tupuwilda: him-weed-il-I*. This means: I *weeded with him*. All similar situations which, wherever possible, we express as aggressive acts, are given as coordinate relationships among the Wintu. The term for what is to us possession or ownership is formed by means of this suffix, from the three kinds of *to be:* in a standing, sitting or lying position. *I have a basket* means really I *live with* or I *sit with a basket*, and is expressed with the same form as that used to say: I live with my grandmother, or I am married to Harry. The term *sukil* which I translated at first as to rule, actually means, to *be-with-in-a-standing-position*, and express the true democracy of the Wintu where a chief stood-with his people.

When the *il* is used as a suffix to a verb, the grammatical object of the verb is particularized for the occasion, and all pronouns and adjectives referring to it are given special suffixes reflective of the coordinate relationships.

There is another suffix, *me*, which also we would translate as transitivizing; and this, I think, even the Wintu would consider as expressive of control, or at least of separation from the self. A man speaking of a man's possessions, in telling a myth, used the *il* and the whole range of particularizing suffixes; a woman telling the same myth, using the same verbs used the *me* instead and left the grammatical object and its attributes in its original generic form. I think the *me* does not contain the respect which is present in the *il*; and its appearance in the texts I have recorded is not frequent.

The Wintu conception of the self then differs from our own in that it contains the total person and the activities of all its aspects, and in that it fades out gradually and without distinct demarcation. It is not clearly opposed to the other, neither is it clearly identical with or incorporated in the other. On most occasions it participates to some extent in the other, and is of equal status to the other; where we see a one way relationship from self to other, an assertion of the self upon the other, the Wintu see a coordinate togetherness, with, at most, a stressed point of view. For example, the phrase I quoted above: *put tupuwilda, I weeded with him,* happens to start with the self; it might have been: *nis tupuwil: he weeded with me.*

This gradually fading involvement of the self in the other can be seen also in the use of the three relational pronouns which are translated in English as *my.* The *neto* refers to objects which I would not hesitate to refer to in terms of the distant or aggressive *me,* and which are spoken of in their generic form. *Netomen* is used for objects for which I am also prepared to use *il.* No *my,* of course, is used for body parts, since these are identical with and not related to the person.

Finally, *net* is used for close relatives as well as acts and states of the self. When referring to close relatives, the *net* is inseparable from the kinship term. Even when referring to an unspecified father, where we would say 'the father' the Wintu says his-father (or her-father). When speaking of *my act* or *my liking* or *my death* or *my destination,* the Wintu separates the *my* from the following word. As I can say *I act* as well as *my act,* so I can also say, *I-younger-sister: I have a younger sister;* and *I-mother: I have a mother* as well as *my fathered: he who has been made into a father by me,* i.e., through my being born. The relatives of this intimate group are treated in the same way as one's acts or state of being.

Linguistic analysis further shows us a different relationship between the self and reality in general from that which is basic to our own culture. The Wintu never asserts the truth as absolute, as we do when we say *it is.* In one of the common stories about the German, the Frenchman and the Englishman, the first two, pointing to bread, say, 'I call it Brot,' and 'I call it pain'; but the Englishman says, 'I call it bread and it *is* bread.' The Wintu never say it *is* bread. They say, 'It looks-to-me-bread' or 'It feels-to-me bread' or 'I-have-heard-it-to-be bread' or 'I-infer-from-evidence-that-it-is-bread' or 'I-think-it-to-be-bread,' or, vaguely and timelessly, 'according-to-my-experience-be bread.' The statement is made about the other, the bread, but with the implication that its validity is limited by the specified experience of the speaker.

For us, that which we sense or know according to man-made rules of logic, is; and that which is beyond my apprehension, beyond my sensing or cognition, is fiction, that is, it is not. The self is the measure of all things. Art and metaphysics and religious experience are barely tolerated on the fringes of our culture. When the fairy godfather first appeared in the Barnaby cartoon, he left a trail of cigar ashes by way of visual proof of his visit. Mysticism is defined negatively as loss of self; and no one in ecstasy is taken seriously, until he comes to his senses. Only when the self is logically and cognitively in control, is experience valid, and except in the arts and religion only that which is ultimately open to such experience is true.

To the Wintu, the cognitive experience of the self is not accorded high status. It must be always documented and is open to question. It is given always through a special derivative stem, usually with a variety of suffixes which make reference to the sensory and other sources of information. However, when the Wintu makes reference to natural necessity, to not-experienced reality beyond man's cognition, he does not document, and he uses the primary form of the stem. Only with the derivative stem does he use assertive suffixes; but here he asserts, not truth, but analyzed experience—perception, cognition, reflection, inference—which is open to question, which is limited by his being, and which need not correspond with the truth. The "mystical" referent alone is accepted without question. And this is true, independent of man's senses and logic.

In other ways, also, we find that with the Wintu the universe is not centered in the self, as it is with us. Take, for example, the term which we use for the individual about whom we are going to speak: ego: I. If the anthropologist wants to make a kinship chart, he starts with ego. If I conjugate, I start with *I run*, and having started with it, I naturally call it the first person; and rightly so, since, in present day English, the third person with its -s suffix is derivative. In Wintu, on the other hand, the third person is primary, and the first is derived. The third person may be represented by the simple stem of experience; or, if a suffix is used, this occurs in the simple stem. The first person is formed derivatively, through suffixation of -*da* to the simple stem or to the suffix.

There is reason to believe, furthermore, that Wintu words are formed on the basis of an outward orientation. They are based on observation, rather than on the kinesthetic experience of the self, or on introspection. Take, for instance, the word for *tick, terus*. It is derived from *tira; to pound to a pulp*. This would mean that *tira* is not concerned with the pounding experience of the self, or with the experience of being pounded, but rather with the shape of the resulting mass. The word for *wade* which is fast disappearing among the bilingual Wintu means: *to-make-a-great-*

splashing-noise. The word *tsiqoha: to-disappear-all-at-once,* is derived from the stem of *tsiqtca,* which means *to be put through a sieve;* that is, to sieve is concerned merely with the observed result of the sieving.

In myths, people are described in terms of the spatial dimension of their activities, observationally. Extremely rarely is there a statement that might be called introspective; such as 'she was furious,' or 'he was happy'; and even here, I am not sure that this is not an observer's statement. The songs the Wintu call love songs refer not at all to the sensations or emotions of love, though they do convey love to us. For example:

> From-Hawk's-scratch-gap
> Downhill-northward-before-you-go
> Oh, look-back-at-me.
> The sleeping place which you and I hollowed out will remain forever.

I have recorded a tale which my informant called a love story. It describes the pursuit of a man by two women who were in love with him. I present a sample of the story:

> They went to the east side of the house, they went around to the east side, and after that they went up the hill to the north, following him running. They went northward at a running pace over the north flat, wishing to see the man who had gone down the hill northward (the word for wish also means to try). And the man was not there but there lay his tracks going forward. And they ran, they went at a running pace, they went rapidly. And at the South-slope-climb, when they came in full view of the north, they looked northward but they did not see him.

The Wintu use of *left* and *right,* as compared with ours, shows again the difference in orientation. When we go for a walk, the hills are to our right, the river to our left; when we return, the hills change and the river, while we remain the same, since we are the pivot, the focus. Now the hills have pivoted to the left of me. This has been English practice for many years, since at least the fourteenth century. To the Wintu, the terms left and right refer to inextricable aspects of his body, and are very rarely used. I think that only once the term left occurs in my texts, referring to a left-handed mythical hero; I cannot remember any occurrence of the term for the right. When the Wintu goes up the river, the hills are to the west, the river to the east; and a mosquito bites him on the west arm. When he returns, the hills are still to the west, but, when he scratches his mosquito bite, he scratches his east arm. The geography has remained unchanged, and the self has had to be reoriented in relation to it.

I said in the beginning of this essay that I should have written from society as the starting point, or at any rate from what we consider the not-self. I came to this conclusion partly on the basis of the material which I have presented here, partly through my experience in recording an autobiography. When I asked Sadie Marsh for her autobiography, she told me a story about her first husband, based on hearsay. When I insisted on her own life history, she told me a story which she called, 'my story.' The first three quarters of this, approximately, are occupied with the lives of her grandfather, her uncle and her mother before her birth; finally, she reaches the point where she was 'that which was in my mother's womb,' and from then on she speaks of herself, also.

In conclusion, I should like to state that the two different conceptions of the self need not be regarded as mutually contradictory. I believe that they can refer to the same absolute truth, and can be said to give us clues to this truth.

REFERENCES

Lee, Dorothy. "Conceptual Implications of an Indian Language." *Philosophy of Science* 5:89-102 (1938).

————. "The Place of Kinship Terms in Wintu Speech." *American Anthropologist,* 42:604-616 (1940).

————. "The Linguistic Aspect of Wintu Acculturation." *American Anthropologist,* 45:435-440 (1943).

————. "Categories of the Generic and the Particular in Wintu." *American Anthropologist,* 46:362-369 (1944).

————. "Stylistic Use of the Negative in Wintu." *International Journal of American Linguistics,* 12:79-81 (1946).

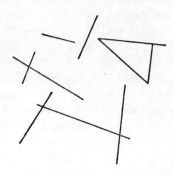

View of the Self
in Greek Culture

FOREMOST IN THE GREEK'S VIEW OF the self is his self-esteem. It is impossible to have good relations with Greeks unless one is aware of this, the Greek *philotimo*. It is important to pay tribute to it, and to avoid offending it, or as the Greeks say, molesting it. Everyone has his *philotimo*, as an individual, as a member of a family, and, most of all, as a Greek. On this rests Greek individualism, since it is sheer being which is respected here, not position in the world or achievement. On this rests Greek democracy and equality, since everyone, both as a person and as a Greek, is equal in his *philotimo* to everyone else, neither superior nor inferior. Any Greek bootblack is equal to the king, to whom he may refer familiarly as *coumbaros*, wedding sponsor, until some political agitator points out to him that the king is not Greek by descent, and therefore does not merit loyalty or respect as an equal. This does not mean that there is lacking a balance of roles or interpersonal structuring; but these relationships of interdependence, of leader and followers, of division of areas of responsibility and work, are not cast in the mold of superiority and inferiority. Inferiority comes only with the forfeiting of the *philotimo*.

From *Cultural Patterns and Technical Change*, a manual prepared for the World Federation of Mental Health, UNESCO, 1953.

On the *philotimo* also rests Greek nationalism. A man may be ignorant and poor, but when his country is threatened, it is his right and privilege to shed his blood on the altar of Greek freedom along with every other Greek, whatever his district, however wealthy or educated. Again, he shares with every other Greek a common glorious past. A small island, speaking of its illustrious sons, lists the New York chiropractor of today next to the philosopher of 2,400 years ago. A Greek, speaking about his culture, makes statements such as: "The Greeks have been hospitable since the time of Homer." Even learned treatises, such as a paper on present-day medicine, may begin with the glorious work of the ancient Greek thinkers. This is what each Greek esteems in himself, what constitutes his *philotimo*: his personal being, his status within a family, village, district, and, second to none, his Greekness.

The Greek *philotimo* is easily bruised, or molested; and a Greek addressed in a completely objective manner, or hearing himself or his way of life described in harsh scientific terms, is greatly offended. Where an American journalist or scientist, writing about his culture, feels the need to be objective, to uncover the facts, a Greek presents each fact wrapped in some subjective, protective covering. The fact is true and dependable, but it should not be naked. A memorandum of fact by a Greek is full of such phrases as: "Then the nobleness of the Greek soul was revealed," or "The Greek peasant modestly died . . . to protect his beloved country, but his death was one of the noblest sacrifices to the idea of liberty." Or, if Greeks have to criticize, they do it with oratory also, reviling passionately, as when a mother scolds a loved one with fury but not with cold and calculating anger.

The covering of the naked fact is essential to the integrity—the absence of all molestation—of the *philotimo*. The inner core of the Greek must never be exposed; and *entrope*, the Greek word for shame, modesty, decency, propriety, self-consciousness, embarrassment, means: "turning inward." This is a concept both positive and negative: you have done something shameful only because you have failed in the positive aspect, in modesty and decency. Out of *entrope*, a Greek avoids saying things and doing things which would reflect on the *philotimo* of himself, his family, his country. For example, the self-made man in Greece does not boast of his rags-to-riches progress. This would expose the poverty of his village, the inability of his family to help him, the fact that his uncle or his godfather could not or did not do his duty by him; it would expose much that should remain decently covered, and would further prove him to be lacking in *philotimo*.

The Greek *philotimo* should not be confused either with the notion of face or with that of pride. Pride for the Greeks carries with it the connotation of arrogance: "the proud bird is caught by the nose." A Greek mother is not proud of her son: she is honored by him; the *philotimo* is enhanced through honor, not pride. There is something of the notion of face, in that it is insupportable to have one's failures and needs known. But there is more than this; what is really bad is that you yourself should expose your failure or yourself. And you have no *philotimo* if you avoid going to fight for your country, whether anyone knows this or not.

The essence of *philotimo* is inviolability and freedom. The first means that a Greek is very "touchy." In a very popular work of the thirties, which gives a humorous report of the cases in the Court of Petty Offences, a large proportion of the cases arise out of this molestation of the *philotimo*. The reaction is immediate, either in scathing invective, such as name-calling, or as physical attack. Offence against one's *philotimo* brings retaliation, not self-reproach. There are suicides in Athens for financial reasons, or for love, but none are reported as a result of a molested *philotimo*.

Freedom is the positive aspect of this. Greeks say: "To be a Greek means to be free," and "Nothing is beautiful unless you are free, not even the flowers in the spring." It gave the Greeks a great sense of freedom to defy Hitler, in the sure knowledge that their country would be overrun and occupied if they did so. During the occupation, they remained free; little children risked their lives to do absolutely unnecessary things such as defacing Nazi posters, giving expression to their essential freedom. The morale of the people was upheld by their knowledge that they had not forfeited their freedom, and that they had been defeated only technically, not man-to-man, but by monstrous machines. External coercion without internal submission has no bearing on the maintenance of the *philotimo*.

The image of the self includes that of the body and of the personality: the person. Life is structured and experienced according to the rhythm and patternings of the body, and ethics is defined by personal relationships, loyalties and roles, just as society is structured according to the physiological relationships of the body. The imagery which a lover uses to describe the body of his beloved is that which is used to praise the personal qualities of an adored leader.

There is no reference to softness in any of the personal folk songs of the Greeks, the dystichs directed toward a loved one, the lullabies, the dirges composed for a relative. The beloved is commonly likened to a tree, sometimes to a fruit tree, but most commonly to a cypress—slim, straight, tall, hard, resistant—"I embrace a cypress tightly," sings a lover. The body is likened to hard, cold substances. The neck of the beloved is made of crystal; the breasts are of marble, in the rare references found in impersonal folk songs. A lover sings: "All night I lay embracing gold."

Firmness and straightness are extremely desirable personal qualities. Babies are swaddled to keep them from going crooked and to make their backs firm. The gesture of mother love is one of holding a firm, stiff, straight bundle against the breast, not the crooking of the arms to accommodate a cuddling body. Firm and straight also is the ideal personality. Parents are urged to be firm of will with their children from birth, and to see that the children develop steadfastness. When Eleutherios Venizelos died, the leading Athenian newspaper wrote: "The cypress is fallen."

Cold, also, is attractive as well as admirable. To call a girl "cold water" is to call her attractive and desirable. Coldness and flowers are on a par in the folk songs, and lovers walk together among the flowers, or on snowy slopes. Hotness means a lack of control, unthinking response. Grief is hot, and tears wither the grass and trees they water. Love as suffering also burns: a lover sighs and 3,000 trees burn up. It is common for a passing youth to say to a girl, "You burn my heart."

The body image is the image of the Greek character. Fortitude and hardihood, firm will, a love of simplicity in food, entertainment, furnishings, the standard of living in general, are common traits. The "good" man will smoke only a few cigarettes a day, drink within measure and eat in moderation; excess is disliked. Fortitude is an ever-present quality; the *philotimo* brooks no calculation of danger or pending pain before a step is taken. If a thing is worth doing, the price to be paid for it is irrelevant; and you are able to do it because you are strong and firm. You do not even ask yourself ahead of time whether you have the necessary fortitude; a Greek takes no inventory of himself because from the time he was a baby, his parents saw to it that he grew straight and hard, and because he knows himself to be a Greek. A current book on child care warns parents not to take many toys to a sick child, not to clown for his amusement, lest this spoil him. Going to bed also is a sign of weakness except for recognized disease. A man cannot seek solace in bed for fatigue or indisposition, lest he appear to be giving in to a desire for pampering. Even to fall asleep is phrased as giving in; the term is "sleep caught me."

It is difficult to give this picture attractively, to show how there is warmth within this firmness, exuberance within the austerity, and within the discipline. Yet discipline is a positive, liberating, guiding element in the Greek personality: the simple life is a joy and is also freeing, since it creates few demands, few dependencies on the external. Self-discipline and self-control are not prohibiting; they are incentive. They are not the application of discipline to the self, but rather a way of behaving.

There is nothing inconsistent with these traits when, in voting on an important issue by roll call, a member of parliament answers, "Five thousand times, yes," or when white pigeons are released in the House by the victorious party. This is appropriate exuberance, just as the fiery reaction to a violation of the *philotimo* is appropriate and within the channel of discipline. There is joy and dignity in hard work, not compulsiveness; there is joy in walking an hour and a half to and from the field twice a day over difficult ground. American visitors are taken for a walk by a young Greek village girl or even a child, and return exhausted. There is a revelling in sheer exertion, in sheer fortitude. There is nothing grim about it, neither is there boasting. Greeks may boast about their achievements, but not of their character, which they take for granted as Greek.

The organs of highest significance are the eyes. They are the seat of the person. With them, lovers and friends communicate, and they are the pre-eminent medium of enjoyment. Love comes through the eyes, and the eyes are mentioned the most frequently in the personal poems. "We have not seen you" means "We missed you."

In the folk songs, a beloved's eyes shoot arrows, strike with a poisoned sword, catch a man in a net, they burn the heart or break it into pieces; they lead astray, they bewitch, they destroy. Glances are rarely sweet, and never soft or gentle, in the love dystichs. Here eyes are always black, perhaps because one is apprehensive if they are blue, the color of the evil eye. It is difficult to overestimate the joy of sheer vision. The folk songs are full of the beauty of flowers and meadows and streams, of the sea with its fleet of sailboats, of the blue of the sky. In villages and towns, the people go strolling after work is done, calling this not a promenade, but *syryani*, "enjoyable viewing." When a long-absent loved one is returning, people congratulate, saying: "Light for your eyes."

Next to the eyes come the lips, but, red and sweet though they be, they are primarily important because of the words which come out of them. Like the eyes, they lead astray not through making false promises, but by engendering love. Speech is of extreme importance to the Greeks, since it establishes and fosters the all-important personal relationships. Almost everyone creates songs; love songs at the village festival, dirges, lullabies, songs of the way of life, songs of work, songs of one's village and of nature.

It is important to find the graphic word in the most ordinary speech, and to turn a spicy phrase. Utterance will take the form of a small oration without creating self-consciousness; an answer is often incisive repartee. There are orations in the coffee house, and wherever a few people gather together. Even learned papers or scientific journals, when not under foreign influence, are often couched in oratory. *Couvenda,* conversation, is a recognized form of "passing the time," of entertainment, perhaps on a par with *syryani. Couvenda* is rarely desultory, or the mere exchange of information. It is usually contrapuntal virtuosity, incisive, combative, loud; and loudness is such a familiar quality of conversation that radios are turned on much too loud for the ears of foreigners. A statement or a question is countered by a challenging question. Tact and gentleness have no part here, insults are hurled, attacks are made, within the appropriate limits. A discussion is a battle of personal opinion, and its end is neither to reach the truth nor to reach a conclusion; its end is sheer enjoyment of vigorous speech.

The hair is a focus of erotic attraction. In the folk songs there is often the picture of a girl letting her hair down as a ladder hung for her lover. For the man, the moustache is a symbol of his manhood and attractiveness. The beard is not important, and in a folk song, a priest's wife calls her husband a bearded goat. A man without face hair is called a *Spanos,* and is a figure of derision in the folklore, and sometimes of fear.

Beyond the features of the head, very little of the body is mentioned in the personal folk songs. Genital organs must never be mentioned, and many women know no names for them. Out of over 400 love couplets analysed, only one mentions the breast, "your breast is like Paradise." Formally, as a general division of the body—as the chest—the breast is named in the same way for men and women and the term can be used freely. In its sexual aspect of a female breast it must not be mentioned, as none of the sexual areas are mentioned. Its functional term, however, the nursing-breast, *vyzi,* is commonly used without embarrassment and when a mother is nursing, there is no embarrassment about exposing the breast for suckling.

The sense of smell is extremely important to the Greeks. In the personal folk poems, there is much mention of sweet-smelling flowers, herbs, trees: "musk and cinnamon, a beautiful girl she is" says a rhyming game. An unexpected guest will be offered a "smell" of whatever the housewife is cooking, or the family is eating. And it is smell which makes the cravings of a pregnant woman not to be denied. A neighbor automatically puts aside a bit of her cooking to send to the pregnant woman next door; and in a grocery store, a customer often offers a "smell" of the olives she has bought to a pregnant customer.

Orderliness is a highly valued quality. Love songs mention the orderly hair, the orderly teeth. The most recent book on child care lays great stress on avoiding the disordering of a child's teeth and facial contours, giving several sketches and photographs of wrong ways of laying the child in bed or postures in sitting at a school desk which might lead to crookedness, and detailed descriptions of specific distortions and their causes. In houses which contain only one room, areas of work and living are carefully specified and maintained through scrupulous order. The Greek equivalent of "set to rights" or "all right" or "under control" is "in order."

The covering of the *philotimo* and the covering of the naked fact find their counterpart, if not their basis, in the body. The body is never naked or, perhaps, only when absolutely necessary. Mothers often arrange to bathe and change the baby without undressing it all at once. The new pediatric practices and the new books on child care demand immersion, but it is all a matter of hygiene; no joy in the naked baby is mentioned anywhere. Conversely, dress, and particularly festive dress, "dress of splendor" and ornamentation, are of great importance, and in fact, are essential to complete the body. When beautiful girls are described, their clothing and their jewelry are given at least as much place as their bodily charms, and are not treated separately; and when a brave youth, a *pallicari*, is mentioned, his trappings are part of the picture. Jewelry and brilliant clothes, woven with gold and silver thread, figure largely in the lullabies, as well as in the love songs and wedding songs. And the lower world which holds no joy is a place where there are no ornamental trappings. The naked body, like the naked word, is stark and grim and incomplete.

The body and the self, the Greek person, delimit, pattern and give shape to relationships and experience. All relationships start with the body and continue along lines of physiological relatedness. They are extended along lines of concrete personal contact. Greeks travel, but mainly along a chain of personal relationships; they go to see a friend of a relative of a friend, and the end, however distant, is concretely linked through persons with the original person. Progress is amelioration of the concretely experienced, or the benefit of immediate relatives or friends or linked persons. The new can be introduced, not for the benefit of mankind or even the Greeks, but for the benefit of people along related lines, and better still, it can be introduced by a known and respected intermediary.

Figures on a chart mean very little to Greeks, and when they refer to people, may even be offensive. Foundations, such as the Near East Foundation, which have recognized this, have been successful in their relations with Greeks and in the introduction of desirable changes. They realized that they had to use not impersonal scientists but people who were primarily leaders, with scientific knowledge, people who were willing to go and live in the villages, and make the acquaintance of the peasants over coffee in coffee houses. And the villagers fell in with the proposals for new hygienic methods and child care and artificial insemination because they had respect for and faith in the man who made the proposals. And where schemes introduced in the name of self-interest did not succeed, those introduced in the name of respected leader did.

"For your sake" is a common sanction. Greek families receiving CARE parcels impersonally, make great efforts to attach a person to the name of the sender; they often write very personal letters, trying to send photographs of themselves, "so that you can see us." In Greece there are no political bosses, since a man's vote is too personal, too much bound by personal loyalty, to be swayed by self-interest. On the other hand, we do find demagogues, who by sheer oratory and force of personality can inspire loyalty to themselves, and thereby, to their ideas. If there are irregularities at the polls, they generally come about not through the selling of one's vote, but through an attempt to vote several times in an impassioned effort to ensure the election of the chosen candidate.

Greek ethical conduct is personal also. A plea in the name of humanity or of kindness is meaningless to most Greeks; and only recently, in Athens, which has been affected by foreign ideas, did a plea in the name of the suffering peasants find true response. An organization called Friends of the Village was formed, and the aid given is by specific persons to specific people or families, in terms of a personal relationship. A peasant woman, writing to such a "Friend" in Athens, accepts the gift with ease and gratitude saying: "You are now my sister, and your family is my family."

Americans, who excel in impersonal kindness, are always surprised to see their human, warm, generous Greek friends remain unmoved and unresponsive in the face of suffering strangers. Greeks, on the other hand, are surprised to see their kind American friends giving according to figures on a piece of paper, according to what they can afford. In giving, Greeks deprive themselves of the very necessities of life, impoverish and even bankrupt themselves; but they recognize their responsibility to give only where personal relations are involved.

This is also true where truthfulness, honesty, loyalty and obedience are concerned. Greek parents are agreed that the principal thing to teach their children is to be honest and to tell the truth; but this, of course, means to be honest in their dealings with their parents and other relatives and all the friends of these, and with people who value them and trust them as persons. Honesty in abstraction is not a virtue, and may even be branded as foolishness. Loyalty also is never to something abstract, like the government, which is equated with impersonal law. Loyalty is to the Greek nation, to Greece, the mother of the people, to personified freedom, but not to "the Greeks" who are unknown. Profiteering and dealings on the black market were not considered bad, because they circumvented only impersonal law and showed disloyalty only to the government and to the unknown Greeks; actually they were good in terms of the family, to whom an individual owes his loyalty.

Responsibility is not social responsibility but family responsibility, or it might be extended to friends and to the village. With loyalty evoked only in personal relations, it follows that Greeks cannot be impartial in awarding jobs or distributing goods. To take care of one's own first, irrespective of merit or of an order of priority, is one's duty; it means fulfilling one's role. Yet impartiality, just because it is so difficult to maintain in the face of strong forces and temptations to "bend," and devotion to an abstract ideal of honesty, just because it is saintly, are highly admired in Greece—though perhaps not by the immediate relatives of the impartial man. Such people inspire what amounts to worship.

Cooperation in this framework is actually mutual aid, one person helping the other, or it is loyalty to the leader who initiates a cooperative undertaking, with men contributing their work for his sake, and women bringing gifts to him, which can be used incidentally for the undertaking.

Obedience is very important and is taught to a child almost from birth; but again, this is obedience within a structured whole, to the parents, older siblings, and to people who stand in this relationship; that is, to friends of the parents or of older relatives, or appropriately introduced older people. Authority comes only from a place in this structured whole, and obedience is only to people. Government is not personal, and the law is external to the organic, structured whole. It is not the voice of Greece. There is therefore no obligation to obey the law; the guide to conduct here is expediency, and the ability to circumvent. Before the political centralization, there was obedience and lasting loyalty to the schoolteacher. Now he represents only the interfering authority of the government, and it is an accepted thing that the students should try to circumvent his authority in every way they can, playing tricks on him and otherwise treating him as an enemy, since he is outside of the web of their loyalties.

Attitudes towards work, time, planning and spending arise also from the person or body as pattern and definition.

Work is life for the Greek. It is the person in function. Things like sports, weekends and vacations, or like "leisure" in the Western sense, are the recent introductions of foreigners. There are times when work or certain kinds of work are interdicted, but this is part of religion, not a claim to leisure time or idleness. And leisure is an attitude, a dimension of all work, and in fact, of all life; it is not confined to a time of day but is the constant expression of internal freedom while at work or at rest.

Diligence is part of the image of the self; it is a personal quality warmly admired. To call a girl *procommene*, diligent, is to say something about her attractiveness. A poem which school children used to memorize spoke of the joyous little housewife, the little girl who got up early to set the house in order. There was nothing of the repellent goody-goody about her, and nothing strange about calling industriousness joyous. The Greek folk songs, often sung as accompaniments to the dance, picture such work situations: a group of young girls laundering at the beach, spreading the clothes and playing in the sand; or the woman singing at her loom. Folk tales make cruel fun of the lazy wife who comes to grief.

Visitors to Greek villages bring back a picture of busy, happy life, of the girls and women gossiping at the fountain in the village square as they wait their turn; of the mother weaving in the shade of the grape arbor while she watches the food cooking on the outdoor brazier, of her daughters working beside her and the little children running about, playing or running errands; of husband and wife walking to the fields an hour or so away, the little children running by their side, the swaddled baby hanging stiffly at the mother's hip, swinging with every step. To some extent, this may be the romantic view of the city-dweller; but it does show the a picture of shared family work as the medium of family life, as the way in which the growing child comes to belong to and identify himself with the unit of his birth.

Diligence is an internal attitude; it rests on self-discipline and free incentive, it includes interest and enjoyment. It does not mean a valuation of work for its own sake; it is the personal quality of diligence, not work itself, which is good. To work compulsively is to be a slave to work; and what can be worse than slavery? Even to work under the compulsion of work as a virtue is to deny oneself prized freedom; all work under pressure, such as the pressure of a time limit or the dictates of an employer, means loss of freedom. Industrialization and work in urban centres usually run counter to this value. Greeks who emigrated to the United States to earn money for their sisters' dowries, or for land needed by the family, worked incredibly long hours, but neither through external nor through inner compulsion. They worked at their own shoeshine booths, or their own fruit-stands or restaurants; they took on unfamiliar occupations such as cooking, rather than submit to an employer.

Greeks "pass" the time; they do not save or accumulate or use it. And they are intent on passing the time, not on budgeting it. Although city people say that this picture is changing, that they are now made aware of the need to use time, the attitude is still widely prevalent, even in the area of private life among the urban groups.

The clock is not master of the Greek: it does not tell him to get up, to go to the field. In many villages, in spite of recent changes, the peasants still get up at sunrise or dawn to go to the fields, and return at sundown. The day is made for work. At night women visit and gossip; men join them or go to the coffee house; there is story-telling, and ardent political discussion; and as for any work done after dark, "the day takes a look at it and laughs." Wherever there is no law to the contrary, a man opens his store in due course, not by the clock; however, in the cities he now functions under clocked time because he comes under government and union regulations.

It is distasteful to Greeks to organize their activities according to external limits; they are therefore either early or late, if a time is set at all. At church the people are not impatient while waiting for Mass to begin; and the church fills only gradually. They know when to go to church; yet when a foreign visitor inquires as to the time of a certain Mass, the subject creates a discussion; and eventually the answer will be something like: "Between 2 and 3." And when Greeks who follow their traditional ways invite, they say, not: "Come at 7 o'clock," but: "Come and see us." To arrive to dinner on time is an insult, as if you came just for the food. You come to visit, and the dinner eventually appears. Among urbanized Greeks, this custom now seems burdensome, and there are many cartoons on the subject.

The dinner is not planned to appear at a predetermined time; and the housewife does not cook by the clock. She tells by the smell or the consistency, or the color, or the resistance against the stirring spoon, or the passing of time is gauged by the intervening activities. Greek men and women work expeditiously, as a rule, but do this best at their own rhythm; any need to hurry is external and interfering; it introduces fuss and disturbance. Efficiency can usually be found when it is not a conscious end.

To introduce an awareness of time into a meal is particularly abhorrent to Greeks, though this has to be done where factories set time limits. Traditionally, dinner is served when it is ready, and without regard to efficient consumption. The fish is not fileted, the nuts are not shelled, the fruit is not sliced. The eater will spend a long time removing infinitesimal bits of flesh from the head of a small fish. All this is part of the process of eating, which is more than the naked act of consumption. He will end his meal with an orange which he will peel with virtuosity, leaving the peel in one piece; to consume an orange in the form of juice is to take all the meaning out of the act.

Greeks in the city, in some circles, find the need of hurry entering their lives. They are not at home with it. For the Greek traditionally, to work against time, to hurry, is to forfeit freedom. His term for hurry means, originally, to coerce oneself. A visitor arriving out of breath may say: "I have hurried," but the form in which the term is more often used is "Don't hurry." One does not admonish another to coerce himself, and a mother does not constantly ask her child to hurry up, unless perhaps she is following some new book on child training which says that a baby must not be allowed to set his own pace. But a Greek has other linguistic ways of expressing expeditiousness. There is the gentle hint: "Won't you make speed?" There is the reassuring "I have finished," meaning "I am coming to the end as fast as I can," and there is the urgent call for help: "Arrive!"

There are many clocks and watches in Greece now, both in the city and the village. Watches are an important part of a man's trappings, and of a girl's adornment. Clocks are necessary to complete the furnishing of a house. If they are in good running order, and are in use, their function is one of reference; they do not shape the household life. They give information and satisfy curiosity. However, there are exceptions to this, particularly among the few mothers who follow the child training directions for rigidly scheduled feedings and bedtime. Villagers speak of hours and minutes, but these are merely references to the passing of time, rather than its measure. Visitors, asking how far it is to the next village, find that "five minutes" may mean half an hour or two hours, but they find that the answer "A cigarette away" does provide reasonably accurate measure.

In spite of the prevalence of timepieces, the church bell and the school bell, and even a cannon blast, continue to have active functions in calling adults or children to pre-arranged gatherings or communal village work. Even in the cities, people are called "Englishmen" when they turn up on the dot at meetings or appointments. People often arrive an hour late to an appointment to find that the other person is also just arriving, or, if they find him gone, they usually accept the fact with neither apology nor frustration.

REFERENCES

Abbott, G. F. *Macedonian Folklore*. Cambridge: Cambridge University Press, 1903.

Allen, Harold B. *Cover Over into Macedonia*. New Brunswick: Rutgers University Press, 1943.

Charitaki, Koste *To Vivlio tes Meteras (The Book of the Mother)*. Athens: Petrou Demetracou, 1948.

Garnett, Lucy M. *Greek Folk Poesy*. London: David Nutt, 1896.

Gray, Peter *People of Poros*. New York: Whittlesey House, McGraw-Hill Book Company, 1942.

Karmoule, Georgiou I. "Tragoudia Kretika" (Songs of Crete). *Laographia*, 9, no. 1-2. Athens, 1926.

Kazave, Georgiou N. *Nisyrou Laographica (Folklore of Nisyros)*. New York: Diury, 1940.

Kokkolatos, N. C. and C. N. Kokkolatos *Dia tas Nearas Meteras (For the Young Mothers)*. Athens: A. A. Papaspyrou, 6th ed., 1947.

Morgenthau, Henry *I was sent to Athens*. Garden City: Doubleday Doran, 1929.

Polites, N. P. *Eclogae apo ta Tragoudia tou Ellenicou Laou (Selections from the Songs of the Greek People)*. Athens: Estia, 1914.

Psatha, D. E. *Themis Echei Kephia (Themis Enjoys Herself)*. Athens: Demetracou, 1937.

Schriver, Joanne Lee *Notes on the Culture of the Greeks of Nisyros*. (MS.), 1947.

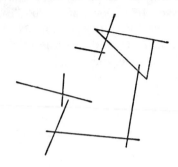

Cultural Factors

in Dietary Choice

FROM THE VERY FIRST, INGESTION for the human being is culturally structured. Is the infant put to the breast, or given the bottle? Will his first suckling be that of colostrum, or of milk, or of some other fluid? Will he be held in a fetal position as he suckles, cradled in naked contact with a mother who curves herself around him, experiencing simultaneously comfort, social warmth, solace, emotional communication and nutrition? Or will he experience his first feeding held in meticulous sanitation against the starched bosom of someone to whom he is merely a case with a name, of someone who regards and expresses this situation as one of sheer nutrition? These questions are answered differently according to the culture of the society into which the infant is born.

The first experience of solid food will differ according to the culture. If he is a Tikopia, he will get premasticated food, warmed with the mother's body warmth and partly digested through her salivary juices; his mother will put it directly to his mouth with her lips. If he is in our society, he will get this food with a hard metal spoon, introduced into a mouth which has never experienced anything so solid or hard, into which not even

From *The American Journal of Clinical Nutrition*, No. 2, March-April 1957, Vol. 5.

teeth have yet erupted. In all this, the culture enters into the food experience, shaping, emphasizing even choosing the significant factors for defining the experience. In our own society, we define it—at least academically—as nutrition. Other societies may emphasize the aspect of social sharing to such an extent that nutrition and even the search for satiety may become secondary.

Culture may present food as mainly the means for the stilling of hunger, or of getting nutrition or as the way to psychosomatic health; it may regard eating as a duty or a virtue, or as gustatory pleasure, or as a social or a religious communion. It is difference in the cultural structuring of the food situation which has made it possible for the people in one urban society to bolt unpalatable food at a quick-lunch counter, while the men of another society, fully as urban, have been prepared to close shop for two hours at noon for the sake of having a leisurely meal at home with their families. The emphasis on the family meal may be so great as to overshadow other aspects. In Athens, during the last war, when the population was starving and cold, soup kitchens were set up by the Red Cross so as to give the people one hot meal a day in a heated room. However, many people asked to be given the food to take home, where they could eat it cold, in a cold room, as a family group. Some of us, in this country, go to great lengths of deprivation and discomfort so as to be able to eat Thanksgiving dinner with our families.

An instance of almost exclusive emphasis on the social aspect of the situation of ingestion is found among the Arapesh of New Guinea, as described by Margaret Mead. Here food, in its entire process, from production or gathering to consumption, is regarded primarily as a medium for social warmth and intercourse; and this view of food affects the nutritional pattern, as it makes for gross inefficiency in food production from our point of view.

The Arapesh in question live in a mountainous area, so rugged that there is almost no level land, and the small garden plots may be separated by miles of difficult territory from the hamlet. The most economical way to cultivate them would be by one gardener working alone; yet up to six men may work on a small plot, with their wives and children, traveling over forbidding territory from plot to distant plot, enjoying each other's society and the sharing of work. "The ideal distribution of food" writes Margaret Mead—"is for each person to eat food grown by another, eat game killed by another, eat pork from pigs that have been fed by people at . . . a distance." So a man walks miles with his coconuts to plant them on the sites of others, he gives his pigs to relatives in distant hamlets to feed and tend for him, he hunts only to give his kill away, since the lowest form of humanity is the man who eats his own kill, even one tiny bird. Thus it is ensured that every mouthful the Arapesh consumes has been the medium of social participation.

Here the Arapesh makes a choice which affects his nutrition. His land is thin, his bush inhospitable; the work of getting food very arduous. Yet, instead of concentrating his energies upon procuring all the food possible, the Arapesh dissipates them (or perhaps concentrates them) on the business of including all the social warmth possible within the total food situation. Margaret Mead calculated that an Arapesh spends about a third of his time in highly energy-consuming travel, which, from a rationalistic point of view is entirely unnecessary.

As a result of all this, the Arapesh are undernourished by our standards. Their daily diet consists of less than half of what the government of New Guinea has specified as the minimum for plantation laborers whose life, we gather, is not more arduous than that of the mountain Arapesh at home. Yet, because of their cultural values, these people choose to spend a large proportion of their energy and time on aspects of food that have nothing to do with hunger or nutrition; in fact, if there is "dietary choice" here, it is the choice of malnutrition. The lives of these people however belie undernourishment. They live and work happily and reproduce themselves. Mead gives pictures of men walking many miles over very rugged territory to and from their gardens, and working hard when there; of women proudly carrying loads of seventy pounds up and down steep mountain sides.

There are many societies in the Pacific which resemble the Arapesh in their approach to the entire food process; societies such as that of the Trobrianders, among whom the main part of the yam harvest was given to the brother-in-law, ideally to function only as a gift and to rot eventually uneaten. These are societies where the exchange of food does not mean the introduction of variety but rather of social intercourse. We have societies where the custom of sharing special or excess food influenced diet in other ways; for example, it meant that no methods of meat preservation were necessary, as with the Ifugao of Luzon, where animals were slaughtered only for sacrifice, and the flesh of a large animal would be distributed to all—thus assuring periodic feasts of meat to rich and poor alike.

In considering an individual's reaction to the food he eats, the factor of culture has again to be taken into account. What will whet the appetite, what will bring a feeling of satiety, what is tasty, depends on the particular culture of the individual in question. The Ifugao of Luzon were reported to eat sweet potatoes without pleasure; what aroused their appetite was rice. People in the Middle East cannot achieve satiety unless they have eaten bread—with or without accompanying food.

Even what is recognized as food depends on the culture. We do not regard dragonflies as human food; the Ifugao do. They eat three species of dragonfly, as well as locusts which are boiled, then dried, then powdered and stored for food. They eat crickets and flying ants which they fry in lard. They eat red ants and water bugs and a variety of beetles. I doubt that I would recognize these insects as food, however hungry I might be. On the other hand, I regard milk as food, a fluid which some cultural groups regard with disgust, as akin to a mucous discharge.

My culture decides, furthermore, in what form I shall consume my food. As a child in a Greek community, I either drank my milk hot after boiling, or, more frequently, I ate it in the form of cheese or yaourt, but never in the form of cream sauce or an ingredient of bread, as I do in this country. I ate my oranges complete with all the inner skin; I never drank them, nor ate the segments divorced of their covering. I ate my fruit raw almost always, whether fresh or dried. The food I ate might be regarded as greasy by people of this country, but my bread was never covered by grease, as it is here; except on few occasions it was innocent of all butter.

Attempts to introduce the boiling of water in the interest of public health in a Peruvian village met insuperable resistance because this changed the classification of water from "cold" food to "hot" food; and "hot" food was appropriate only to specific situations. In this area, to understand dietary choice, to understand preparation of food and the planning of specific menus, it is essential to understand the principle of "hot" and "cold" foods in reference to each state of the body.

My culture tells me *when to have an appetite for what.* When I get up in the morning, I have no appetite for roast fresh ham or cold cuts of sausage; but I do have one for fried smoked ham and fried sausage. For me, this is an appetite acquired gradually over a period of thirty years; before that, according to my Greek urban culture, I would have found ham or eggs or sausages for breakfast revoltingly heavy, whereas I had an appetite for bread and cheese at this time of day. Whether I shall satisfy my appetite or not depends—beyond the economic factor—on culture. Millions of women in this country who have an appetite for rich desserts, for cream in their coffee, for butter on their toast, forgo these items in the interest of a slender appearance. We have societies where young marriageable women stuff themselves with equivalent items because their culture sets a value on plumpness.

According to our culture, also, we decide which part of the plant or animal to eat: leaves, or flower, or stalk or root; muscle and liver, or the entire animal, including spleen and lungs and intestines, eyeballs and cheeks. Or, according to the culture again, we may have no choice. For example, among the Zulu of South Africa, when a sacrificial ox is killed, a year after the death of the head of the family, the entire kin group assembles and each individual is given a prescribed part of the ox, according to age, sex, and relationship to the family; need or personal preference are not taken into account.

The cultural influence on food selection may be indirect, representing a value which pervades all areas of living. For instance, in this country monotony of diet has been found to work against appetite. This I believe, is related to the general American value of the new, of change, of variety. We have societies, however, where what is valued is sameness; where monotony is good and sought. And we have societies where the appearance of the staple is necessary and welcome at every meal. A Greek regards bread as appetizing at all meals as well as at snack time; and in this country, where meals often end in sweet desserts, many Greeks take a bite of bread at the very end. Bread has been eaten with every mouthful of food up to dessert; the dessert has been an interruption, a variation of the "monotony," which the eater now proceeds to eliminate, thus leaving the table with the taste of bread in his mouth. In addition, no variety is sought in the kind of bread eaten.

In this country, the emphasis laid upon speed and efficiency throughout the culture has affected dietary choice, for example through transforming oranges into orange juice, and introducing the sandwich lunch; and the sandwich form itself is a factor in selecting food.

The kind of food appropriate to different occasions during the year, to different days of the week, to different hours of the day, is culturally patterned also. The food of Lent among Orthodox and Catholic Christians, limited to fish and dairy products and vegetable foods, or only to vegetable products; the lamb on Easter or the ham; the Christmas goose; the Thanksgiving turkey; the Sunday dinner; the special Friday evening meal of the Orthodox Jews; the Bairam lamb preceded by the day-long fasts of the Ramadan; duty days of the Buddhist Burmese which provide festive fare every eight days, and the slim period of the Buddhist Lent which covers one-fourth of the year—all these dietary "choices" are made for the individual by his culture.

The force of the dietary patterning varies in the list I have given above. No lamb at Easter may mean only a lack of joy and satisfaction; but lamb accidentally ingested during Lent may mean acute dysphoria to the devout, a sense of sin and perhaps illness. It would be an infringement of a religious food taboo, and these taboos are a potent selective factor, whether they cover the year or a season, whether they cover a lifetime or a stage of life as with the Murngin of Australia where only men who are fathers can eat porcupine, emu eggs, snake eggs, crayfish and a number of other items.

Informants from other societies have reported that they chose starvation rather than infringement of a food taboo—though they obviously lived to tell the tale. Schweitzer gives cases where individuals unwittingly broke a food taboo and died within a day. Such interdictions sometimes deprive individuals of the very food they require. Among the Zulu milk can never be eaten by pregnant or lactating or menstruating women, and preferably never at all past pubescence, as the reproductive function of woman is inimical to the welfare of cattle, and might somehow reach and harm the cattle through the medium of their milk. Besides, people can consume only the milk of the cattle belonging to their own family line, and since women spend their adult lives in the kraal of a different family line, that of the husband, they cannot have milk even when they are not engaged in the reproductive function.

A cultural factor of great importance is expressed in the symbolic aspect of food: in its value to the individual over and above satiation or nutrition. During the last war, after the invasion of the continent, the newspapers announced that whole turkeys had been sent to France for the Thanksgiving celebration. This, at a time when all conveyance was needed for the last tremendous war effort, gives some clue to the symbolic significance of turkey at Thanksgiving to Americans—not turkey meat, but a whole turkey, to be seen and carved. If the turkeys did arrive, I am sure they contributed strongly to Allied victory. The same turkeys, however, would have been nothing but so much poultry flesh to Greeks or Yugoslavs or Turks at this time, much inferior to mutton.

To people throughout the Middle East, bread is truly the staff of life, having a significance which verges on the religious. In the Egyptian village described by Ammar it is profane to put bread on the ground, all fallen crumbs must be picked up lest they be stepped upon, and any bread that falls on the ground must be kissed before it is removed from harm's way. Here a man heard with horror the tentative suggestion that one could have a meal without bread; and Ammar tells of two women who were divorced by their husbands, mainly for seldom providing them with fresh bread. Here, as in many areas of the Middle East, without bread a meal is impossible, because bread itself is the meal and all "food" is only an accompaniment, something to dip the bread in, or a relish; and satiety, as I mentioned above, cannot be found without bread.

The place which bread holds in the Middle East is held by corn among the Indians of the Southwestern United States and of Mexico; and attempts to enrich the diet in Mexican villages have had to deal with the unshakable place which corn holds in the life of the peasants. In this country, the Hopi say: "Corn is life and piki the perfect food;" and certainly true Hopi life cannot go on without corn. Traditionally, corn functions as food, but this is only one of its functions. No child can be born with security, nor live through the first hazardous twenty days of life, without corn; in fact corn is needed ritually at every step throughout life. The entire process of growing and harvesting and living with corn, in fact, is necessary to a valid and meaningful life, since the entire religious cycle of ceremonials is bound with the growing cycle of the corn. In the face of this, "free" rational dietary choice, based on nutritional requirements biochemically determined, has little chance.

Any attempt to affect diet must deal with the cultural factors in dietary choice. It may come to grief against the symbolic value of the food involved. More than this, it must take into account what it is that the food situation mediates, so as not to destroy a source which it cannot replace with sheer nutrition.

REFERENCES

Ammar, Hamed *Growing Up in an Egyptian Village, Silwa, Province of Aswan.* London: Routledge & Kegan Paul, Ltd., 1954.

Barton, R. F. *Ifugao Economics.* University of California Publications in American Archaeology & Ethnology, 15, no. 5:385-446 (1922).

Cassel, John "A Comprehensive Health Program Among South African Zulus." In Paul, B. (ed.) *Health, Culture and the Community.* New York: Russell Sage Foundation, 1955.

Firth, Raymond *We, the Tikopia.* New York: American Book Company, 1936.

Goldman, I. "The Ifugao of the Philippine Islands." In Mead, M. (ed.) *Cooperation and Competition Among Primitive Peoples.* New York: McGraw-Hill Book Company, 1937.

Malinowski, Bronislaw *Coral Gardens and Their Magic.* New York: American Book Company, 1935.

Mead, Margaret *Sex and Temperament in Three Primitive Societies.* New York: William Morrow & Company, 1935.

————. "The Arapesh of New Guinea." In Mead, M. (ed.) *Cooperation and Competition Among Primitive Peoples.* New York: McGraw-Hill Book Company, 1937.

————. *The Mountain Arapesh I. An Importing Culture.* Anthropological Papers of the American Museum of Natural History, 36: pt. 3 (1940).

————. *The Mountain Arapesh II. Socio-Economic Life.* Anthropological Papers of the American Museum of Natural History, 40: pt. 3 (1947).

Schweitzer, Albert *African Notebook.* New York: H. Holt & Company, 1939

Simmons, Leo W. *Sun Chief.* New Haven: Yale University Press, 1942.

Thompson, Laura and Alice Joseph *The Hopi Way.* Chicago: University of Chicago Press, 1944.

Warner, W. L. *A Black Civilization, A Social Study of an Australian Tribe.* New York: Harper & Brothers, 1937.

Wellin, E. "Water Boiling in a Peruvian Town." In Paul, B. (ed.) *Health, Culture and the Community.* New York: Russell Sage Foundation, 1955.

The Religious Dimension

of Human Experience

IN PRIMITIVE SOCIETIES, WE DO NOT always find the worship of God or a god, nor the idea of the supernatural. Yet religion is always present in man's view of his place in the universe, in his relatedness to man and nonhuman nature, to reality and circumstance. His universe may include the divine or may itself be divine. And his patterned behavior often has a religious dimension, so that we find religion permeating daily life—agriculture and hunting, health measures, arts and crafts.

We do find societies where a Supreme Being is recognized; but this Being is frequently so far removed from mundane affairs, that it is not present in the consciousness of the people, except on the specific occasions of ceremonial or prayer. But in these same societies, we find communion with the unperceivable and unknowable in nature, with an ultimate reality, whether spirit, or power, or intensified being, or personal worth, which evokes humility, respect, courtesy or sometimes fear, on man's part. This relationship to the ultimate reality is so pervasive, that it may determine, for example, which hand a man will use in adjusting his

From *Religious Perspectives in College Teaching*, ed. Hoxie N. Fairchild. The Ronald Press Company, New York City, 1952.

loin cloth, or how much water he will drink at a time, or which way his head will point when he sleeps, or how he will butcher and utilize the carcass of a caribou. What anthropologists label "material culture," therefore, is never purely material. Often we would be at least as justified to call the operation involved religious.

All economic activities, such as hunting, gathering fuel, cultivating the land, storing food, assume a relatedness to the encompassing universe, and with many cultures, this is a religious relationship. In such cultures, men recognize a certain spiritual worth and dignity in the universe. They do not set out to control, or master, or exploit. Their ceremonials are often periods of intensified communion, even social affairs, in a broad sense, if the term may be extended to include the forces of the universe. They are not placating or bribing or even thanking; they are rather a formal period of concentrated, enjoyable association. In their relationships with nature, the people may see themselves as the offspring of a cherishing mother, or the guests of a generous hostess, or as members of a democratic society which proceeds on the principle of consent. So, when the Baiga in India were urged to change over to the use of an iron plow, they replied with horror that they could not tear the flesh of their mother with knives. And American Indians have hunted many animals with the consent of the generic essence of these—of which the particular animal was the carnal manifestation—only after establishing a relationship or reciprocity; with man furnishing the ceremonial, and Buffalo or Salmon or Caribou making a gift of the countless manifestations of his flesh.

The great care with which so many of the Indian groups utilized every portion of the carcass of a hunted animal, was an expression, not of economic thrift, but of courtesy and respect; in fact, an aspect of the religious relationship to the slain. The Wintu Indians of California, who lived on land so wooded that it was difficult to find clear land for putting up a group of houses, nevertheless used only dead wood for fuel, out of respect for nature. An old Wintu woman, speaking in prophetic vein, expressed this: "The White people never cared for land or deer or bear. When we Indians kill meat, we eat it all up. When we dig roots we make little holes. When we build houses, we make little holes. When we burn grass for grasshoppers, we don't ruin things. We shake down acorns and pinenuts. We don't chop down the trees. We only use dead wood. But the White people plow up the ground, pull up the trees, kill everything. The tree says, 'Don't. I am sore. Don't hurt me.' But they chop it down and cut it up. The spirit of the land hates them. They blast out trees and stir it up to its depths. They saw up the trees. That hurts them. The Indians never hurt anything, but the white people destroy all. They blast rocks and scatter them on the ground. The rock says 'Don't! You are hurting me.' But the White people pay no attention. When the Indians use rocks, they take little round ones for their cooking . . . How can the spirit of the earth like the White man? . . . Everywhere the White man has touched it, it is sore.' "

Here we find people who do not so much *seek* communion with environing nature as *find themselves* in communion with it. In many of these societies, not even mysticism is to be found, in our sense of the word. For us, mysticism presupposes a prior separation of man from nature; and communion is achieved through loss of self and subsequent merging with that which is beyond; but for many other cultures, there is no such distinct separation between self and other, which must be overcome. Here, man is *in* nature already, and we cannot speak properly of man *and* nature.

Take the Kaingang, for example, who chops out a wild bee hive. He explains his act to the bees, as he would to a person whom he considered his coordinate. "Bee, produce! I chopped you out to make beer of you! Yukui's wife died, and I am making beer of you so that I can cut his hair." Or he may go up to a hive and say simply, "Bee, it is I." And the Arapesh of New Guinea, going to his yam garden, will first introduce to the spirit of the land, the brother-in-law whom he has brought along to help him with the gardening. This is not achieved communication, brought about for definite ends. It implies an already present relatedness with the ultimate reality, with that which is accepted in faith, and which exists irrespective of man's cognition or perception or logic. If we were to abstract, out of this situation, merely the food getting or the operational techniques, we would be misrepresenting the reality.

The same present relatedness is to be found in some societies where the deity is more specifically defined. The Tikopia, in the Solomon Islands Protectorate, sit and eat their meals with their dead under the floor, and hand food and drink to them; the dead are all somewhat divine, progressively so as they come nearer to the original, fully divine ancestor of the clan. Whatever their degree of divinity, the Tikopia is at home with them; he is aware of their vague presence, though he requires the services of a medium whenever he wants to make this presence definite.

Firth describes an occasion when a chief, having instructed a medium to invite his dead nephew to come and chew betel with him, found himself occupied with something else when the dead arrived, and so asked the medium to tell the spirit—a minor deity—to chew betel by himself. At another time, during an important ceremonial, when this chief was receiving on his forehead the vertical stripe which was the symbol that he was now the incarnation of the highest god, he jokingly jerked his head aside, so that the stripe, the insignium of the presence of the god, went crooked. These are the acts of a man who feels accepted by his gods, and is at one with them. And, in fact, the Tikopia appear to live in a continuum which includes nature and the divine without defining bounds; where communion is present, not achieved; where merging is a matter of being, not of becoming.

In these societies, where religion is an everpresent dimension of experience, it is doubtful that religion as such is given a name; Kluckhohn reports that the Navaho have no such word, but most ethnographers never thought to inquire. Many of these cultures, however, recognized and named the spiritual ingredient or attribute, the special quality of the wonderful, the very, the beyondness, in nature. This was sometimes considered personal, sometimes not. We have from the American Indians terms such as *manitou*, or *wakan*, or *yapaitu*, often translated as power; and we have the well-known Melanesian term *mana*. But this is what they reach through faith, the other end of the relationship; the relationship itself is unnamed. Apparently, to behave and think religiously, is to behave and think. To describe a way of life in its totality is to describe a religious way of life.

When we speak of agricultural taboos and rites, therefore, we often introduce an analytical factor which violates the fact. For example, when preparing seed for planting, one of the several things a Navaho traditionally does is to mix ground "mirage stone" with the seed. And in the process of storing corn, a double-eared stalk is laid at the bottom of the storage pit. In actual life, these acts are a continuous part of a total activity.

The distinction between the religious and the secular elements may even separate an act from the manner of performance, a verb from its adverb. The direction in which a man is facing when performing a secular act, or the number of times he shakes his hand when spattering water, often have their religious implications. When the Navaho planted his corn sunwise, his act reflected a total worldview, and it would be nonsense for us to separate the planting itself from the direction of the planting.

Those of us who present religion as separate from "everyday" living, reflect moreover the distinctions of a culture which will identify six days with the secular in life and only the seventh with religion. In many primitive societies, religion is rarely absent from the details of everyday living, and the ceremonials represent a formalization and intensification of an everpresent attitude. We have societies such as that of the Hopi of Arizona, where ceremonials, and the preparation for them, cover most of the year. Some years ago, Crow-wing, a Hopi, kept a journal for the period of a year, putting down all events of ceremonial import. Day after day, there are entries containing some casual reference to a religious activity, or describing a ritual, or the preparation for a ceremonial. After a few weeks of such entries, we come to a sequence of four days' entries which are devoted to a description of a ball game played by two opposing groups of children and enjoyed by a large number of spectators. But, in the end, this also turns out to have been ceremonial in nature, helping the corn to grow.

Among many groups, agriculture is an expression of man's religious relatedness to the universe. As Robert Redfield and W. Lloyd Warner have written: "The agriculture of the Maya Indians of southeastern Yucatan is not simply a way of securing food. It is also a way of worshipping the gods. Before a man plants, he builds an altar in the field and prays there. He must not speak boisterously in the cornfield; it is a sort of temple. The cornfield is planted as an incident in a perpetual sacred contract between supernatural beings and men. By this agreement, the supernaturals yield part of what is theirs—the riches of the natural environment—to men. In exchange, men are pious and perform the traditional ceremonies in which offerings are made to the supernaturals . . . The world is seen as inhabited by the supernaturals; each has his appropriate place in the woods, the sky, or the wells from which the water is drawn. The village is seen as a reflection of the quadrilateral pattern of the cosmos; the cornfield too is oriented, laid out east, west, north, and south, with reference to the supernaturals that watch over the cardinal points; and the table altars erected for the ceremonies again remind the individual of this pattern. The stories that are told at the time when men wait to perform the ceremony before the planting of the corn or that children hear as they grow up are largely stories which explain and further sanction the traditional way of life."

Art also is often so permeated with religion that sometimes, as among the Navaho, what we classify as art is actually religion. To understand the rhythm of their chants, the "plot" of their tales, the making of their sandpaintings, we have to understand Navaho religion: the concept of harmony between man and the universe as basic to health and well being; the concept of continuity, the religious significance of the groups of four, the door of contact opened through the fifth repetition, the need to have no completely enclosing frame around any of their works so that continuity can be maintained and the evil inside can have an opening through which to leave.

The sand-paintings are no more art than they are ritual, myth, medical practice or religious belief. They are created as an integral aspect of a ceremonial which brings into harmony with the universal order one who finds himself in discord with it; or which intensifies and ensures the continuation of a harmony which is already present. Every line and shape and color, every interrelationship of form, is the visible manifestation of myth, ritual and religious belief. The making of the painting is accompanied with a series of sacred songs sung over a sick person, or over someone who, though healed of sickness by emergency measures has yet to be brought back into the universal harmony; or in enhancing and giving emphasis to the present harmony. What we would call purely medical practices may or may not be part of all this. When the ceremonial is over, the painting is over too; it is destroyed; it has fulfilled its function.

This is true also of the art of the neighboring Hopi, where the outstanding form of art is the drama. In this we find wonderfully humorous clowning, involving careful planning and preparation, creation of magnificent masks and costumes, rehearsals, organization. Everyone comes to see and responds with uproarious hilarity. But this is not mere art. It is an important way of helping nature in her work of growing the corn. Even the laughter of the audience helps in this.

More than dramatic rehearsal and creation of costumes has gone into the preparation. The actors have prepared themselves as whole persons. They have refrained from sexual activity, and from anything involving conflict. They have had good thoughts only. They have refrained from anger, worry and grief. Their preparation as well as their performance have had a religious dimension. Their drama is one act in the great process of the cyclical growing of corn, a divinity indispensable to man's well being, and to whose well being man is indispensable. Corn wants to grow, but cannot do so without the cooperation of the rest of nature and of man's acts and thoughts and will. And, to be happy, corn must be danced by man and participate in his ceremonials. To leave the religious dimension out of all this, and to speak of Hopi drama as merely a form of art, would be to present a fallacious picture. Art and agriculture and religion are part of the same totality for the Hopi.

In our own culture, an activity is considered to be economic when it deals with effective utilization or exploitation of resources. But this definition cannot be used when speaking of Hopi economics. To begin with, it assumes an aggressive attitude toward the environment. It describes the situation of the homesteader in Alaska, for example, who works against tremendous odds clearing land for a dairy farm, against the inexorable pressure of time, against hostile elements. By his sweat, and through ingenuity and know-how and the use of brutally effective tools, he tames nature; he subjugates the land and exploits its resources to the utmost.

The Hopi Talayesua, however, describing his work on the land, does not see himself in opposition to it. He works *with* the elements, not *against* them. He helps the corn to grow; he cooperates with the thunderstorm and the pollen and the sun. He is in harmony with the elements, not in conflict; and he does not set out to conquer an opponent. He depends on the corn, but this is part of a mutual interdependence; it is not exploitation. The corn depends on him too. It cannot grow without his help; it finds life dull and lonely without his company and his ceremonials. So it gives its body for his food gladly, and enjoys living with him in his granary. The Hopi has a personal relationship with it. He treats it with respect, and houses it with the care and courtesy accorded to an honored guest. Is this economics?

In a work on Hopi economics we are given an account of the Hopi Salt Journey, under the heading, "Secondary Economic Activities." This expedition is also described in a Hopi autobiography, and here we discover that only those men who have achieved a certain degree of experience in the Hopi way, can go on this journey; and then, only if their minds are pure and they are in a state of harmony with the universe. There is a period of religious preparation, followed by the long and perilous journey which is attended by a number of rituals along the way. Old men, lowering themselves from the overhanging ledge onto the salt deposits, tremble with fear, knowing that they may be unable to make the ascent. The occasion is solemnly religious. This is no utilization of resources, in the eyes of the Hopi who makes the journey. He goes to help the growing corn; the Salt Journey brings needed rain. Twelve adult men will spend days and court dangers to procure salt which they can buy for two dollars from an itinerant peddler. By our own economic standards, this is not an efficient use of human resources. But Hopi ends transcend our economic categories and our standards of efficiency are irrelevant to them.

In many societies, land tenure, or the transference of land, operations involved in hunting and agriculture, are often a part of a religious way of life. In our own culture, man conceives of his relationship to his physical environment, and even sometimes his human environment, as mechanistic and manipulative; in other cultures, we often find what Ruth

Benedict has called the animistic attitude toward nature and man, under-lying practices which are often classified miscellaneously together in ethnographies, under the heading of superstitions or taboos. The courteous speech to the bear about to be killed, the offering to the deer world before the hunter sets out, the introduction of the brother-in-law to the garden spirit, or the sacrifice to the rice field about to be sold, the refraining from intercourse, or from the eating of meat or from touching food with the hand, are expressive of such an attitude. They are the practices we find in a democratic society where there is consideration for the rights of everyone as opposed to the brutal efficiency of the dictator who feels free to exploit, considering the rights of none. They reflect the attitude of people who believe in conference and consent, not in coercion; of people who gener-ally find personality or mana in nature and man, sometimes more, some-times less. In this framework, taboo and superstitious act mean that man acts and refrains from acting in the name of a wider democracy which includes nature and the divine.

With such a conception of man's place in nature, what is for us land tenure, or ownership, or rights of use and disposal, is for other societies an intimate belongingness. So the Arapesh conceive of themselves as be-longing to the land, in the way that flora and fauna belong to it. They cultivate the land by the grace of the immanent spirits, but they cannot dispose of it and cannot conceive of doing so.

This feeling of affinity between society and land is widespread and appears in various forms and varying degrees of intensity, and it is not found only among sedentary peoples. We have Australian tribes where the very spirit of the men is believed to reside in the land, where a bush or a rock or a peculiar formation is the present incarnation of myth, and contains security and religious value; where a social class, a structured group of relatives, will contain in addition to human beings, an animal and a feature of the landscape. Here, when a man moves away from the land of his group, he leaves the vital part of himself behind. When a magistrate put people from such societies in jail in a distant city, he had no idea of the terrifying severity of the punishment he was meting; he was cutting the tribesman off from the very source of his life and of his self, from the past, and the future which were incorporated and present in his land.

In the technology of such societies we are again dealing with material where the religious and secular are not distinct from each other. We have, for example, the description which Raymond Firth gives of the replacing of a worn out wash strake on a canoe, among the Tikopia. This operation is expertly and coherently carried out, with secular and religious acts performed without distinction in continuous succession or concurrently. A tree is cut down for the new wash strake, a libation is poured out to the deities of the canoe to announce this new timber, and a kava rite is performed to persuade the deities to step out of the canoe and on to a piece of bark cloth, where they can live undisturbed, while the canoe is being tampered with. Then comes the unlashing of the old wash strake, the expert examination of the body of the canoe in search of lurking defects, the discovery of signs indicating the work of a borer, the cutting of the body of the canoe with a swift stroke to discover whether the borer is there, accompanied by an appeal to the deities of the canoe by the expert, to witness what he is doing, and the necessity for doing it.

Now a kinsman of the original builder of the canoe, now dead and a tutelary deity, spontaneously drops his head on to the side of the canoe and wails over the wounding of the body of the canoe. The borer is discovered, in the meantime, to be still there; but only a specially consecrated adze can deal with him successfully. The adze is sent for, dedicated anew to the deity, invoked, and finally wielded with success by the expert.

All this is performed with remarkable expedition and economy of motion yet the Tikopia workers are not interested in saving time; they are concerned neither with time limits nor with speed in itself. Their concern is with the dispossessed deities whose home must be made ready against their return; and the speed of their work is incidental to this religious concern. The end result is efficiency; but unlike our own efficiency, this is not rooted in the effort to utilize and exploit material and time resources to the utmost; it is rooted in that profound religious feeling which also gives rise to the time-consuming rites and the wailing procedures which, from the purely economic point of view, are wasteful and interfering.

The world view of a particular society includes that society's conception of man's own relation to the universe, human and non-human, organic and inorganic, secular and divine, to use our own dualisms. It expresses man's view of his own role in the maintenance of life, and of the forces of nature. His attitude toward responsibility and initiative is inextricable from his conception of nature as deity-controlled, man-controlled, regulated through a balanced cooperation between god and man, or perhaps maintained through some eternal homeostasis, independent of man and perhaps of any deity. The way a man acts, his feeling of guilt and achievement, and his very personality, are affected by the way he envisions his place within the universe.

For example, there are the Tiv of Southern Nigeria who as described by one of them in the thirties, people the universe with potentially hostile and harmful powers, *the akombo*. Man's function in the maintenance of his own life and the moderate well-being of the land and of his social unit, is to prevent the manifestation of *akombo* evil, through performing rites and observing taboos. So his rites render safe through preventing, through expulsion and purging. His role is negative, defending the normal course against the interference. Vis-a-vis the universe, his acts arise out of negative motives. Thus what corresponds to a gift of first-fruits to a deity in other cultures, is phrased as a rite for preventing the deities from making a man's food go bad or diminish too quickly; fertility rites for a field are actually rites preventing the evil-intentioned from robbing the fields of their normal fertility.

In the writings of R. F. Barton, who studied the Ifugao of Luzon in the early part of this century, these people also appear to see deities as ready to interfere and to bring evil; but their conception of man's role within the structure of the universe is a different one from that of the Tiv. In Barton's descriptive accounts, the Ifugao either accept what comes as deity-given, or act without being themselves the agents; they believe that no act can come to a conclusive end without the agency of a specific deity. They have a specific deity often for every step within an operation and for every part of the implement to be used. R. F. Barton recorded the names of 1240 deities and believed that even so he had not exhausted the list.

The Ifugao associate a deity with every structured performance and at least a large number of their deliberate acts. They cannot go hunting, for example, without enlisting the aid of the deity of each step of the chase, to render each effective, or to nullify any lurking dangers. There is a deity for the level spot where "the hunter stands watching and listening to the dogs"; one for when the dogs "are sicced on the game," one for when "the hunter leans on his spear transfixing the quarry"; twelve are listed as the deities of specific ways of rendering harmless to the hunter's feet the snags and fangs of snakes which he encounters. If he is to be successful in the hunt, a man does not ask the blessing of a deity. He pays all the particular deities of every specific spot and act, getting them to transitivize each act individually.

Even so, in most cases an Ifugao remains non-agentive, since the function of many of the deities is to save man from encounter, rather than to give him success in his dealing with it. For example, in the area of interpersonal relations, we have Tupya who is invoked so that, "the creditor comes for dun for what is owed, but on the way he forgets and goes about other business"; and Dulaiya, who is invoked so that, "the enemies just don't think about us, so they don't attack." His tools, also, are ineffective of themselves; so that, when setting a deadfall, he invokes and bribes such deities as that for the Flat Stone of the Deadfall, the Main Posts of the Deadfall, the Fall of the Deadfall, the Trigger of the Deadfall. Most of the Ifugao economy is involved in providing sacrifices to the deities, big or little according to the magnitude of the operation and the importance of the deities. There is no warmth in the sacrifices; no expression of gratitude or appeal or belongingness. As the Ifugaos see it, the sacrifice is a bribe. With such bribes, they buy the miraculous intervention and transitivization which are essential for achievement, health, and good personal relations.

The Ifugao show no humility in the face of this ineffective role in the universe; they merely accept it as the state of things. They accept their own failures, the frequent deaths, the sudden and disastrous flaring up of tempers, as things that are bound to happen irrespective of their own desires and efforts. But they are neither passive nor helpless. They carry on great undertakings, and, even now they go on forbidden head-hunts. They know when and how and whom to bribe so as to perfect their defective acts. When however, a deity states a decision, they accept it as immutable. A Catholic priest tells a story about the neighboring Iloko which illustrates this acceptance. A Christian Iloko was on his deathbed, and the priest, trying to persuade him to repent of his sin, painted to him vividly the horrors of hell; but the dying man merely answered, "If God wants me to go to hell, I am perfectly willing."

Among the Wintu Indians of California we find that man sees himself as effective but in a clearly limited way. An examination of the myths of the Wintu shows that the individual was conceived as having a limited agentive role, shaping, using, intervening, actualizing and temporalizing the given, but never creating; that man was viewed as needing skill for his operations, but that specific skill was useless without "luck" which a man received through communion and pleading with some universal power.

It is to this limited role of man, geared to the working of the universe, that I referred when I spoke earlier of Hopi drama and agriculture. Without an understanding of this role, no Hopi activity or attitude or relationship can be understood. The Hopi have developed the idea of man's limited effectiveness in their own fashion, and have elaborated it systematically in what they call the "Hopi Way." Laura Thompson says of the Hopi, "All phenomena relevant to the life of the tribe—including man, the animals, and plants, the earth, sun, moon, clouds, the ancestors, and the spirits—are believed to be interdependent . . . In this system each individual—human and non-human—is believed to have . . . a definite role in the universal order." Traditionally, fulfillment of the law of nature—the growth of the corn, the movements of the sun—can come only with man's participation, only with man's performance of the established ceremonials. Here man was effective, but only in cooperation with the rest of the phenomena of nature.

The Indians of the Plains, such as the Crow and the Sioux, have given a somewhat different form to this conception of man's circumscribed agency. The aggressive behavior for which they have been known, their great personal autonomy, their self-assurance and assertiveness and in recent years, their great dependence and apathy, have been explained as an expression of this conception. These societies envisioned the universe as pervaded by an undifferentiated religious force on which they were dependent for success in their undertakings and in life generally. The specific formulation differed in the different tribes, but, essentially, in all it was believed that each individual and particularly each man, must tap this universal force if his undertakings were to be successful. Without this "power" a man could not achieve success in any of the valued activities, whether warfare or the hunt; and no leadership was possible without this power. This was a force enhancing and intensifying the being of the man who acted; it was not, as with the Ifugao, an effectiveness applied to specific details of activities. The individual himself prepared himself in the hardihood, self-control, skills and areas of knowledge necessary. Little boys of five or seven took pride in their ability to withstand pain, physical hardship, and the terrors of running errands alone in the night. The Sioux did not appeal for divine intervention; he did not want the enemy to forget to come. Yet neither was he fearless. He appealed for divine strength to overcome his own fears as well as the external enemy.

The relationship with the divine, in this case, is personal and intense. The Plains Indian Sioux did not, like the Hopi, inherit a specific relatedness when he was born in a specific clan. Each man, each pre-adolescent boy, had to achieve the relationship for himself. He had to go out into the wilderness and spend days and nights without food or drink, in the cold, among wild beasts, afraid and hungry and anxious, humbling himself and supplicating, sometimes inflicting excruciating pain upon himself, until some particular manifestation of the universal force took pity upon him and came to him to become his life-long guardian and power. The appeals to the universal force were made sometimes in a group, through the institution of the Sun Dance. But here also they were individual in nature. The relationship with the divine was an inner experience; and when the Dakota Black Elk recounted his autobiography, he spoke mainly of these intense, personal religious experiences. Within this range of variation in form and concept and world view, we find expressed by all the same immediate relatedness to the divine.

REFERENCES

Barton, R. F. "The Religion of the Ifugao." *American Anthropological Association Memoirs*, No. 65, 1946.

Black Elk Speaks. Being the Life Story of a Holy Man of the Oglala Sioux, as told to John G. Neihardt (Flaming Rainbow). New York: William Morrow & Company, 1932.

Brown, Joseph Epes. *The Sacred Pipe, Black Elk's Account of the Seven Rites of the Oglala Sioux*. Recorded and edited by Joseph Epes Brown. Norman: University of Oklahoma Press, 1953.

Firth, Raymond. *The Work of the Gods in Tikopia*. London: Lund, Humphries & Company, Ltd., 1940.

————. *Primitive Polynesian Economy*. New York: Humanities Press, 1950.

Henry, Jules. *Jungle People*. New York: J. J. Augustin, Inc., 1941.

Redfield, Robert and W. Lloyd Warner. "Cultural Anthropology and Modern Agriculture." *Farmers in a Changing World, 1940 Yearbook of Agriculture*. Washington, D. C.: United States Government Printing Office.

Thompson, Laura. *The Hopi Crisis*: Report to Administrators. (Mimeograph) 1946.

Vanoverbergh, Morice. *The Isneg Life Cycle*. Publication of the Catholic Anthropological Conference, 3, No. 2, 1936.

Index

175

TWENTIETH CENTURY VIEWS

American Authors

TWENTIETH CENTURY VIEWS

European Authors